ONE FOR THE POT

ONE FOR THE POT

by Ray Cooney and Tony Hilton

Warner Chappell Plays

LONDON

A Warner Communications Company

First published in 1963
by Warner Chappell Plays Ltd.,
(pka English Theatre Guild Ltd)
129 Park Street, London W1Y 3FA.

Second edition 1975
Third edition 1990

ISBN 0 85676 033 1

Typeset and printed by Commercial Colour Press, London E7.

ONE FOR THE POT was produced by Rix Theatrical Productions at Whitehall Theatre, London on 2 August, 1961, with the following cast:

CHARACTERS IN ORDER OF APPEARANCE

AMY HARDCASTLE	Sheila Mercier
CYNTHIA HARDCASTLE	Helen Jessop
JUGG	Leo Franklyn
JONATHAN HARDCASTLE	Terry Scott
CLIFTON WEAVER	Peter Mercier
ARNOLD PIPER	Larry Noble
CHARLIE BARNET	Basil Lord
HICKORY WOOD	Brian Rix
WINNIE	Hazel Douglas

GUESTS: *Jeanne Cook, Robert Checksfield, Pearson Dodd, Stuart Sherwin, and Gerald Dawson*

The Play Directed by Henry Kendall

Setting by Rhonda Grey

Lighting by Gilbert Harrison

* * * * * *

Originally produced at the Richmond Theatre on 2 November, 1959, with the following cast:

JUGG	Ivor Salter
CYNTHIA HARDCASTLE	Hazel Douglas
JONATHAN HARDCASTLE	Malcolm Russell
CLIFTON WEAVER	Aubrey Woods
ARNOLD PIPER	Derek Tansley
CHARLIE BARNET	Raymond Dyer
HICKORY WOOD	Ray Cooney
WINNIE	Edna Hopcroft

Produced by Jack Williams

Description of Characters

Billy Hickory Wood — A shy, lovable North Country lad.

Rupert Hickory Wood — A well-spoken young man who, when agitated, gets tongue tied.

Michael Hickory Wood — An unscrupulous but likeable Irish rogue.

Pierre Hickory Wood — A volatile Frenchman.

(*Note:* The above four characters are all played by one actor with the assistance of doubles.)

Charlie Barnet — A middle aged cockney full of humour and guile.

Jugg — The butler. Born in Stepney but now considers himself an h'upper class servant.

Jonathan Hardcastle — A North Country mill owner. Irascible in temper and hard drinking in habit. He does his best to hide his native generosity.

Cynthia Hardcastle — Hardcastle's attractive daughter. Full of life and fun.

Amy Hardcastle — Hardcastle's unmarried sister. She is a maidenly lady left over from the Edwardian era.

Arnold Piper — A humourous solicitor who holds an unspoken admiration for Amy.

Winnie — Billy's North Country wife.

Clifton Weaver — A suave, charming art critic.

HICKORY WOOD AND DOUBLES

Authors' Notes

At the Whitehall Theatre three identical doubles were used but this is not necessary and the following is recommended:

The parts of BILLY, RUPERT, MICHAEL and PIERRE can be played by the principal actor and one double. This double should be approximately the same build and within an inch of the principal actor's height. This double will make all on-stage appearances.

Two other doubles are required but as they only appear briefly when falling out of the cocktail cabinet in Act III and previously in Act II, when their arms and legs are seen, they need only to be approximately the same height.

It is recommended that the doubles have red wigs and the principal actor has a matching red rinse. Or that wigs are obtained to match the principal's own hair colour.

For the majority of the play all HICKORY WOOD's are wearing evening dress. BILLY wears his jacket undone, his cloth cap and his hair flopping over forehead. RUPERT is immaculate, his hair neatly combed. MICHAEL wears his jacket undone and smokes a pipe.

When the double is on stage he must only appear and move with his back to the audience, but this is sufficient for the illusion. It is also recommended that the double studies most carefully the different 'walks' of the principal actor in his parts of BILLY, RUPERT, and MICHAEL. This will help to make the illusion complete.

For BILLY's first entrance the principal actor wears grey trousers, raincoat, scarf and cap. He is underdressed in evening suit ready for RUPERT's first entrance.

For MICHAEL's first entrance (Act III) he puts trousers and overcoat over evening suit.

In Act III when MICHAEL is imitating BILLY his Yorkshire accent is very broad and overdone.

PRODUCTION NOTES

The action throughout the play takes place in the lounge of Jonathan Hardcastle's country house near London on one mad Midsummer's Night.

The action is continuous.

The room is on the ground floor and it is light and comfortable.

The main feature of the set is the large fireplace alcove up centre. This has panelled walls and the lower half is masked by a large wing armchair with its back to the audience in front of the fireplace. Right of the armchair and flush to the upstage wall is a large movable screen and left of the armchair a small table.

There are three entrances visible to the audience into the room:

(1) *Hall:* Stage right of the fireplace alcove, on an oblique angle, is a curtained archway leading to the rest of the house. Upstage is the front door and ballroom. Downstage to the living quarters.

(2) *Library:* Below the archway is a door, opening upstage, leading to the library.

(3) *French Windows:* The french windows are set stage left of the fireplace alcove.

Downstage left of the french windows is a large cocktail cabinet set into the wall. This is not a piece of furniture but a small cupboard which has been redesigned as a cocktail cabinet, it should be large enough to hold two people. When the door opens upstage this displays on the door a bottle rack and a small shelf for glasses.

The furniture is good, but neither modern nor antique. Below the cocktail cabinet down left is a bureau with trick drawer, operated from behind flat so that it can be pushed open by the stage management. On this is a large old-fashioned gramophone with a detachable horn, assorted records, vase of flowers and ashtray.

On the wall above the bureau is a pedestal on which stands a small bust of a woman.

Downstage right of the library door and flush to the wall is a refectory table, covered with a full length white table-cloth and party dressing.

Between the french windows and the fireplace up left, is a large chest, on which is draped a large Spanish-type shawl.

There is an armchair, with footstool set right centre with a small table on two levels left of it.

A large round settee stands left centre with cushions on it. A small stool stands downstage of refectory table down right.

The telephone is on the small table left of the wing chair. On the walls down left and down right are a number of paintings and drawings.

There are crossed swords (Practical) above the chest up left and a hanging warming pan (Practical) downstage of the library door. There is a carpet runner downstage of the wing armchair.

As it is night the room is lit mainly by four double wall-brackets in fireplace alcove. Similar brackets are placed above refectory table down right and bureau down left. The switches are downstage of library door. There are fairy lights strung to the portico outside the french windows and two candelabras on refectory table down right.

There are four concealed exits and entrances on the stage:

(1) Through the downstage flat of the fireplace alcove, which is masked by the wing armchair and screen.

(2) Under the refectory table, which is masked by a hanging tablecloth.

(3) Through the back of the chest.

(4) Through the back of the cocktail cabinet.

(See Ground Plan)

(Directions are *Stage* Right and Left)

from the Everyman Theatre, Cheltenham production of One for the Pot

ACT ONE

The curtain rises, the doorbell rings twice as AMY HARDCASTLE *comes in from hall upstage carrying a large birthday cake which she places on refectory table down* R. *The doorbell rings again.*

AMY (*Calling.*) Jugg? Oh, dear, Jugg?

(*She goes to Hall Upstage and calls off.*)

Jugg! Jugg!

(CYNTHIA *enters from french windows carrying easel and canvas.*)

CYNTHIA (*Calling.*) Jugg? Where is Jugg? He's never here when he's wanted. We'll never be ready at this rate.

(*Doorbell rings again.* CYNTHIA *crosses to archway.* AMY *re-enters hall upstage.*)

CYNTHIA Aunt Amy, have you seen Jugg?

AMY Cynthia, dear, have you seen Jugg?

CYNTHIA I haven't seen him all evening.

AMY Oh, dear. It's time you were changing, Cynthia. Your guests are beginning to arrive. I've told them to use your father's study as a cloakroom.

CYNTHIA I've put the musicians in there.

AMY I thought Jugg was seeing to all this. I told your father twenty years ago he should never have hired him. Now, where was I–? (*Doorbell rings.*) Oh, dear–

CYNTHIA All right, auntie, I'll go.

AMY Yes–and see if you can find Jugg. Maybe he's helping cook in the kitchen.

CYNTHIA He's more likely kissing her in the pantry.

AMY Cynthia!

(CYNTHIA *exits hallway upstage.*)

AMY Oh, dear, maybe I'd better go and look.

(AMY *exits hallway downstage.*)

(*Off.*) Jugg–Jugg!

(JUGG'S *smiling face appears from behind wing chair up* C. *He has an empty brandy glass in his hand.*)

JUGG Ha, Ha. Many were called but few answered. Ha, Ha. That's a nice drop of stuff. I think I'll have a drop more.

(*He finishes it and crosses to cocktail cabinet down* L. *He looks furtively around and then helps himself to another drink. Then he tries the bureau drawer, finding it locked. He steps back a pace and stamps on the floor–the drawer flies open.* JUGG *takes out a cigar and sniffs it appreciatively. He takes a swig at his drink as* AMY *re-enters from hall downstage.*)

AMY Jugg!

(JUGG *chokes on his drink and, in one movement, bangs the drawer closed with one hand and tips the brandy into flower vase with the other.*)

AMY Jugg, what are you doing?

JUGG I was just watering the flowers, Miss Amy.

AMY Go and get changed and see to Miss Cynthia's guests.

JUGG (*Moving to hall.*) Yes, Miss Amy.

AMY And tell the musicians to start as soon as they're ready.

JUGG Yes, Miss Amy.

AMY And phone Davis's and see what's happened to my present for Miss Cynthia. It hasn't arrived yet.

JUGG Yes, Miss Amy. (JUGG *moves towards the hall once more.*)

AMY — Oh, Jugg–(JUGG *stops.*) Take this into the dining-room. (*She hands him birthday cake from refectory table down* R.) And see that cook's got everything prepared.

JUGG — (*Smiling.*) Yes, Miss Amy.

(JUGG *moves to hallway.*)

AMY — No, Jugg. I'll see cook.

JUGG — Oh! What a pity.

(CYNTHIA *enters hall upstage carrying several coats and wraps.*)

CYNTHIA — Jugg, look after these, will you. (*She puts coats in his arms. To* AMY.) By the way, Daddy's insisting on getting up.

AMY — Oh, no.

CYNTHIA — The doctor's persuaded him to use his wheelchair.

AMY — Oh, dear. I was hoping his gout would keep him in bed until tomorrow. Jugg–

JUGG — (*Resignedly.*) Yes, Miss Amy?

AMY — If Mr. Hardcastle is getting up you're to see he doesn't drink or smoke.

JUGG — That should keep me occupied most of the evening, Miss Amy.

(JUGG *exits into hall downstage.*)

AMY — And if I were you, Cynthia, I'd keep your father away from your artist friends. Remember what happened the last time you had a party.

CYNTHIA — Shall I ever forget.

(AMY *crosses to archway.*)

AMY Jugg, Jugg, take the easel up to the studio and empty those ashtrays.

(AMY *exits hall upstage.* JUGG *enters hall downstage, crosses to easel and places it behind screen.*)

JUGG Empty the ashtrays. Take the easel up to the studio! She'll be lucky.

(JUGG *takes full ashtray off table up centre, goes to empty it under carpet but changes his mind and empties it into chest. Doorbell rings and* JUGG *exits hall upstage.* HARDCASTLE *enters hall downstage in wheelchair. Wheels himself to* C. *stage.*)

HARDCASTLE Ah!

(*Gets out of wheelchair and hobbles over to bureau. Finding it locked.*) Blast! (*He steps back a pace and stamps his foot. It is the gouty one and he lets out a loud cry. He bangs his stick on floor and the drawer flies open.* HARDCASTLE *is lighting a cigar as* JUGG *enters from hall upstage to behind* HARDCASTLE.)

JUGG Ah! Ah! (HARDCASTLE *starts.*)

HARDCASTLE Don't creep about like that, Jugg. Pour me out a brandy.

JUGG Do you think you should, Mr. Hardcastle?

HARDCASTLE Do as I tell you. If my sister found out you spent half your wages at the dog track you'd be out on your ear.

JUGG Very true, sir. On the other hand if she found out you were drinking and smoking you'll be back in bed.

HARDCASTLE Pour us *both* a drink.

JUGG That's better. (JUGG *crosses to cocktail cabinet closing bureau drawer on the way.*) I must confess I need it. (*Pouring drinks.*) There is no question a little brandy comes in handy. (*Crossing to* HARDCASTLE *with drink.*) Your brandy, sir. I suppose you couldn't let me 'ave a small h'advance?

HARDCASTLE No I couldn't.

JUGG Pity–I 'ave a reliable tip for this h'evening's racing–'Flying Jumbo'.

HARDCASTLE Is that a dog or an elephant?

JUGG A dog, sir. Though knowing my luck it'll probably run like an elephant.

HARDCASTLE Oh, well–through the teeth!

JUGG Round the gums!

HARDCASTLE Look out, stomach!

JUGG Here it comes!

AMY (*Off.*) Jonathan!

(*They splutter their drinks.*)

HARDCASTLE Quick, get rid of this!

(JUGG *takes* HARDCASTLE'S *drink and hands him his cigar.* HARDCASTLE *now has both drinks and* JUGG *the cigar.*)

HARDCASTLE No!

(*They try again.* HARDCASTLE *ends up with cigar and* JUGG *with both drinks.*)

HARDCASTLE No!

(*They try again. This time* HARDCASTLE *gets saddled with both drinks and cigar.* JUGG *moves towards cocktail cabinet empty-handed.*)

HARDCASTLE No!

(JUGG *takes* HARDCASTLE'S *cigar and one glass, crosses down* R. *and goes to flick cigar into gramophone horn.*)

HARDCASTLE 'Ere, that's my sister's favourite antique.

JUGG All right, we'll give it to Auntie Flo. (*Places cigar in statuette's mouth which is above bureau and quickly finishes drink.*)

AMY (*Off.*) Are you down there, Jonathan?

(HARDCASTLE *hides his glass under his rug.* AMY *enters hall upstage.*)

AMY How are you feeling, Jonathan? Comfortable?

HARDCASTLE Marvellous.

(AMY *tucks* HARDCASTLE'S *rug in and finds glass.*)

AMY What's this?

HARDCASTLE That quack's medicine–horrible!

(*He goes to drink but* AMY *takes glass, smells it and hands it to* JUGG.)

AMY Put that away, please, Jugg.

JUGG Certainly, madam.

(JUGG *turns away from* AMY *and drinks it as he crosses and puts empty glass in cocktail cabinet.*)

AMY Jugg, did you phone Davis's?

JUGG Oh, yes, Miss Amy. But it was their early closing day.

(*Doorbell rings.* JUGG *exits hall upstage.*)

AMY Oh, dear. Now I haven't got a present for Cynthia.

HARDCASTLE 'Ow about giving her that damned gramophone of yours?

AMY If you can't be civil, Jonanthan, I shall tell the doctor to send you back to bed. And don't forget he told you not to drink or smoke.

(JUGG *enters hall upstage.*)

JUGG Mr. and Mrs. Bowater-Smith.

(JENNIFER BOWATER-SMITH *hurries into the room followed by her husband,* STANLEY. *She is very gushing. He is rather awkward.*)

JENNIFER Mr. Hardcastle! I told Cynthia I simply had to see you. You poor thing. Daddy had gout himself and it made him so miserable. Do you remember me? Of course you do. Jennifer Bowater-Brown. Cynthia and I went to the same art class. Of course I'm Jennifer Bowater-Smith now. You don't know Stanley.

(STANLEY *shakes hand with* JUGG, HARDCASTLE, *and* AMY. *With each handshake* STANLEY *emits a loud 'Ah-ah'.*)

JENNIFER Isn't he sweet? The party's going to be oodles of fun. I was telling Cynthia I must send my eldest to that finishing school. You didn't know I had four little poppets now, did you. Stanley says I've kept my figure, don't you, Stanley. Two girls and two boys. I think that's frightfully clever, don't you. They all take after me. I don't think so but everybody says it. Well, we'll see you in the ballroom. I mustn't let you keep us here chatting. Been lovely seeing. Come on, Stanley.

(STANLEY *shakes hands with* AMY, HARDCASTLE *and* JUGG. STANLEY *repeats his loud 'Ah-ah'.* JUGG *takes his hand away and, wagging his finger at* STANLEY, *says 'Ah-ah'.* JENNIFER *and* STANLEY *exit to hall upstage.*)

HARDCASTLE Well, that were an interesting conversation. How many children did she say she had?

AMY Four, I think.

HARDCASTLE Oh, then, she does stop talking sometimes.

(*The doorbell rings.*)

AMY That'll be more of Cynthia's guests. See to them Jugg.

(*Music is heard in ballroom.*)

JUGG Yes Miss Amy.

HARDCASTLE And keep them arty crafty lot out of here tonight. I've got some business to discuss.

JUGG Yes, sir.

HARDCASTLE And keep that ballroom door shut–And if that damned doctor's still knocking about, tell him I don't want to see him again till the post-mortem.

JUGG Very good, sir.

(JUGG *exits hall upstage*.)

HARDCASTLE (*Shouting*.) His post-mortem.

AMY I think it would have been better if you'd stayed in bed.

HARDCASTLE Oh, do you? Well I've got up to see to some important business. My solicitor's coming to discuss it this evening.

AMY Mr. Piper.

HARDCASTLE Aye, your boy friend.

AMY Jonathan! Mr. Piper's been invited for the party, not to discuss business.

HARDCASTLE Don't worry he'll have plenty of time to flirt with you.

AMY (*Laughing*.) Really–!

HARDCASTLE We're going to settle this Hickory Wood agreement. I had a telegram from Billy Hickory Wood's solicitor. They're coming this evening.

AMY Oh, this is too bad. On Cynthia's birthday.

HARDCASTLE Can't help that, love. It's taken weeks to find Billy Hickory Wood.

AMY Jonathan, I must speak.

HARDCASTLE I know and it's a great pity.

(CYNTHIA *enters hall upstage. She carries a large framed picture which has its back to the audience.*)

CYNTHIA Hello, Poddy. How are you feeling? Are you better? (*She kisses him.*)

HARDCASTLE Stop that nonsense.

CYNTHIA Daddy, there's someone I want you to meet. (CLIFTON WEAVER *enters hall upstage carrying a large suitcase.*) This is Clifton Weaver.

CLIFTON (*With hand outstretched.*) I've heard such a lot about you.

HARDCASTLE I've heard nowt about you.

CYNTHIA Don't mind Daddy, Clifton. His bark's worse than his bite. This is my Aunt Amy.

HARDCASTLE She don't bark or bite.

CLIFTON Charmed.

CYNTHIA I've invited Clifton for the week-end.

HARDCASTLE Oh, have you? (*Sees portrait.*) What's that?

CYNTHIA Clifton's had it framed for me as my birthday present. (*She turns it round and shows the portrait. It is impressionistic and quite ghastly.*)

HARDCASTLE What is it?

CYNTHIA It's my last painting.

HARDCASTLE I should hope so.

CYNTHIA It's a self-portrait.

CYNTHIA Let's hang it shall we?

HARDCASTLE Let's do something to it.

CLIFTON Allow me to help you, my dear.

CYNTHIA (*Crossing down* R.) What about over there, darling?

HARDCASTLE Well, if that don't drive me to drink, nowt will.

(*They hang it above refectory table down* R.)

CLIFTON It might take a little getting used to– (*Expansively.*) You see, it's a new movement in art.

HARDCASTLE Well, the sooner it gets going the better. Any road, what do you know about it?

CYNTHIA Clifton's one of our leading art critics.

HARDCASTLE Oh, is he? Would you like a drink, young man?

(JUGG *enters from hall upstage behind* WEAVER.)

CLIFTON How very kind of you. Have you a gin and French?

HARDCASTLE I said a drink not a ruddy perfume. (*To* CYNTHIA.) Where'd you get *him* from?

CYNTHIA You'd better run along and change, Clifton. Jugg'll show you the way.

CLIFTON Jugg, oh, that's your manservant–he's a queer looking character.

(JUGG *reacts.*)

HARDCASTLE Aye, we seem to attract them round here.

JUGG Mr Piper, your solicitor, to see you, sir.

HARDCASTLE (*To* JUGG.) Send him in.

CYNTHIA Jugg, show Mr Weaver to his room, will you?

JUGG Very good, Miss Cynthia.

CYNTHIA I do apologize, Clifton. My family.

(JUGG *picks up suitcase and hands it to* WEAVER. JUGG *flicks his head as a sign to follow him and exits hall downstage.* WEAVER *follows.*)

CYNTHIA Mr Piper's early, isn't he?

HARDCASTLE Aye. He's panting to whip your Aunt Amy off to Gretna Green.

AMY Oh, Jonathan–you are awful!

HARDCASTLE He's come to settle this Billy Hickory Wood business. Though it'll never be settled if he takes as long about it as he has proposing to your Aunt.

(PIPER *enters from hall upstage carrying brief-case.*)

AMY (*Flustered.*) Mr Piper–

HARDCASTLE Don't stick up for him, He should have marched you down the aisle years ago.

CYNTHIA Daddy look who's–

HARDCASTLE (*With his back to* PIPER.) He's nothing but a long winded, drivelling nincumpoop.

AMY You mustn't talk about the doctor that way.

HARDCASTLE I'm not talking about the doctor. I'm talking about that miserable short-sighted, duck-bottomed old– (*Sees* PIPER.) Hullo Piper.

PIPER Yes, Mr Hardcastle. (*Crossing to* CYNTHIA.) Miss Cynthia, are you having a lovely birthday?

CYNTHIA Yes thank you. Mr Piper. It was very kind of you. I don't go to many parties these days.

(PIPER *sits in armchair down* R.)

HARDCASTLE I'm not surprised. Come on, hurry up.

PIPER No, sir – Yes, sir. (*Reading agreement.*) The agreement for a settlement of ten thousand pounds on William Hickory Wood.

HARDCASTLE That's right.

PIPER Who shall hereinafter be known as the party of the first part by Jonathan Hardcastle, who shall hereinafter–

HARDCASTLE Never mind the psalm singing.

CYNTHIA And who is William Hickory Wood?

HARDCASTLE Billy's father, Samuel were my partner and best friend in Brierly Mill twenty years ago. His son Billy worked for me as a lad.

AMY But ten thousand pounds is a lot of money, Jonathan.

HARDCASTLE It's a pot of money. But Samuel were responsible for success at Mill and the poor old codger dies penniless. I want to repay Samuel by looking after his son Billy. It's the only right and proper thing to do. And besides–I can fiddle it off my income tax. Piper! Is it in there that Billy gets the money providing he's the only living relative of the late Samuel Hickory Wood?

PIPER (*Reading agreement.*) Providing he is the only living relative of the late Samuel Hickory Wood.

AMY But why have you done that, Jonathan?

HARDCASTLE The reason Samuel died a pauper was because his idle shiftless relations soaked him for every penny he had. I don't mind giving Billy ten thousand pounds. He were a good lad but a bit slow. Couldn't add two and two together. If any of the other sponging Hickory Woods are still alive they'll go through this money same as they did Samuel's. (*To* PIPER.) What exactly did you put int' newspapers?

PIPER Oh yes, I have a cutting here. (*Referring to press cutting.*) Would any living relative contact you here.

HARDCASTLE Hardly likely the dead uns'll be along.

PIPER And no other Hickory Woods have contacted you?

HARDCASTLE No. Billy and his solicitor are coming this evening. Providing no other Hickory Woods have arrived by tonight he can sign the agreement and I'll hand over the money. Have you got it with you?

PIPER Yes, Mr Hardcastle.

(PIPER *takes a bundle of notes from briefcase.*)

AMY (*Rising, shocked.*) Jonathan, you're not giving the money in cash, surely?

HARDCASTLE I am that!

PIPER Oh, yes. A most deductable item.

(PIPER *puts notes back in briefcase.*)

HARDCASTLE Well make yourself useful. Take my sister along to the ballroom.

PIPER (*Offering* AMY *his arm.*) Delighted I'm sure.

HARDCASTLE And tell them musicians to keep playing.

PIPER Yes.

HARDCASTLE You should be at home among all them fiddlers.

(PIPER'S *smile fades. He and* AMY *exit into hall upstage.*)

CYNTHIA You are awful, Poddy, what would you do without Aunt Amy.

HARDCASTLE Get roarin' drunk.

CYNTHIA You'll never change.

HARDCASTLE I'm all right as I am. If there's anyone to worry about, it's you. Getting mixed up with this lah-de-dah arty types. Can't tell the men from the women half the time.

CYNTHIA Now, Poddy. Don't go on about it.

HARDCASTLE All this nonsense about art.

CYNTHIA I think it's worthwhile.

HARDCASTLE It's worth nowt. You should stay home 'ere. It's about time you settled down.

CYNTHIA Just because you want me to have babies and get married.

HARDCASTLE I do, but not in that order.

CYNTHIA Well. If you're so keen to see me married, you'll be pleased to know that I might get engaged this week-end.

HARDCASTLE Oh, will you–who to?

CYNTHIA He's been leading up to it. Clifton Weaver.

HARDCASTLE Clifton! I'm having none of that.

CYNTHIA I haven't decided what I'll say yet.

HARDCASTLE I don't mind you deciding as long as you say no.

CYNTHIA He's got personality and charm.

HARDCASTLE That's probably the name of the scent he's using. (CYNTHIA *starts to push him towards hall.*) You marry that one and your kids will turn out like one of your paintings.

CYNTHIA And what's wrong with that?

HARDCASTLE If you think I want grandchildren like that–

(*He points to* CYNTHIA'S *painting, as they exit into hall downstage. Doorbell rings.* JUGG *enters from hall upstage and crosses to cocktail cabinet. Helps himself to a brandy. Doorbell rings again.* JUGG *grimaces and finishes his drink. Doorbell again.*)

JUGG Coming! Coming! (*He crosses up* C.)

CHARLIE (*Off.*) Stand close behind me Billy.

(CHARLIE BARNET *enters hall upstage with exaggerated 'posh' walk.*)

CHARLIE (*Entering.*) There was no one at the door. There was welcome on the mat. So we walked right in. Search no more–the beneficiary is found!

(CHARLIE *flicks his fingers.* BILLY HICKORY WOOD *enters hall upstage.*)

May I present Mr Billy Hickory Wood.

(CHARLIE *turns and looks for* BILLY *who has nervously crossed behind him.*)

CHARLIE Billy...?

(CHARLIE *quickly crosses to hall and looks out.* BILLY *follows him up.* CHARLIE *turns again without seeing and crosses to french windows.* BILLY *nervously follows.*)

CHARLIE Billy...?

(BILLY *taps* CHARLIE *on shoulder.*)

CHARLIE Ha, ha, there you are William.

(JUGG *has been watching with amazement.*)

CHARLIE Be so kind as to inform Mr Hardcastle that Mr Billy Hickory Wood is here with Charles Barnet his legal representative.

(CHARLIE *removes his hat with a flourish.* BILLY *repeats it with his cap.*)

JUGG (*To* CHARLIE.) Your things, sir.

CHARLIE (*Giving him briefcase.*) Thank you, my man. (*Giving him umbrella.*) Thank you, my man. (*Giving him scarf.*) Thank you, my man.

JUGG One moment, sir. (*To* BILLY.) *Your* things, sir.

BILLY (*Imitating* CHARLIE–*giving him small handcase.*) Thank you, my man. (BILLY *'feeds' his very long scarf from round his neck straight into the unfurled umbrella.*) Thank you, my man.

JUGG (*Looking at* BILLY'S *cap.*) Don't take your hats off, will you?

BILLY We wasn't going to.

(JUGG *exits hall downstage.*)

CHARLIE Now, Billy, I'm passing meself off as your solicitor.

BILLY What for?

CHARLIE They advertised for you in the paper. They're very likely going to give you a few quid. You've got to be legally represented. Now what's the point of us spending all our money hiring a solicitor, when all I've got to do is put on a posh suit and a bowler hat.

BILLY But we don't know what it's all about. I haven't seen Mr Hardcastle since I worked in his mill as a lad.

CHARLIE (*Showing him paper.*) Why do you think he's gone to all this trouble to find you?

BILLY Perhaps he forgot to stamp my card.

CHARLIE Mr Hardcastle is obviously a man of substance. You've got to make an impression on 'im so for Gawd's sake don't let on you're only a painter's mate in my decorating business.

BILLY Why not?

CHARLIE Well a painter's mate ain't genteel. You can see he's 'rolling' in dough.

BILLY (*Crossing down* L. *to bureau.*) Aye, he must be. Even the statues smoke cigars.

CHARLIE (*Taking cigar.*) Give me that.

(PIPER *enters from hall upstage clutching brief-case.*)

PIPER Oh, excuse me–

CHARLIE Ah, Mr Hardcastle–

PIPER No, I was looking for him myself. (*Holding out hand.*) I'm Arnold Piper, his solicitor.

CHARLIE (*Worried.*) Oh?

PIPER I represent Piper and Morden.

CHARLIE Well, what a coincidence. I represent Barnet and-er-Barnet and-er-er–

BILLY Edgware?

CHARLIE Edgware, No! The good old English firm of Barnet and Cohen.

PIPER Oh, really? Which one are you?

CHARLIE I'm Barnet.

PIPER (*To* BILLY.) Then you must be Cohen.

BILLY No, I've only just arrived.

CHARLIE (*Laughing.*) No, no. You've made a right ricket there. This here is Billy Hickory Wood, that well known beneficiary.

PIPER Oh, how splendid.

CHARLIE Yes isn't it. I'm 'is solicitor.

PIPER (*To* CHARLIE.) I'm surprised we haven't met before.

CHARLIE I've been up north.

PIPER What doing?

BILLY Soliciting.

CHARLIE No, no. Workin' on the case of the-er-Scarlet bedroom.

PIPER Interesting. Where are your chambers?

BILLY In the scarlet bedroom.

(CHARLIE *quickly puts his hat over* BILLY'S *mouth.*)

CHARLIE E's got such a sense of the comical.

HARDCASTLE (*Off.*) In here, you say?

PIPER There's Mr Hardcastle now.

CHARLIE (*To* BILLY.) Watch it, boy, watch it.

(HARDCASTLE *enters from hall upstage.* CHARLIE *pushes* BILLY *forward.*)

HARDCASTLE (*Entering.*) Out of way, Piper. Well, Billy Hickory Wood. (*Seeing* CHARLIE.) I could tell it were you. Who's this?

CHARLIE Charles Barnet, his solicitor,

HARDCASTLE His solicitor, eh? Well, Billy, you've come up in the world since you worked for me. What line of business are you in now?

BILLY I'm a painter.

(CHARLIE *grimaces.*)

HARDCASTLE Not another one! Oh, well, it's a step up from working in't mills. What do you do–oils or water colours?

BILLY I don't do either.

CHARLIE (*Quickly.*) No, he does the lot–oils, water colours–

BILLY Distemper...Whitewash...flatwash...emulsion–

CHARLIE Ha, ha, you'll have to get used to his artistic comical nature.

HARDCASTLE I'm glad he's got a sense of humour. You'll have something in common with my Cynthia. She paints herself.

BILLY 'Ow does she get round the back?

CHARLIE Ha, ha, He's such a card.

HARDCASTLE Right, let's get down to business, shall we?

CHARLIE (*Taking* BILLY *to one side.*) This is it, boy. If he offers a tenner, stick out for twenty.

HARDCASTLE Billy Hickory Wood, I have it in mind to give you ten–

BILLY I want twenty.

HARDCASTLE Ten thousand pounds.

(CHARLIE *chokes.* BILLY *collapses on to his knees.* CHARLIE *pulls* BILLY *up.*)

HARDCASTLE In cash.

(HARDCASTLE *shows them the money as* BILLY *collapses again.*)

HARDCASTLE Providing you're Samuel Hickory Wood's only living relative.

CHARLIE Live, boy, live!

(*He hauls* BILLY *up and walks him wheelbarrow fashion round in a circle round settle until he is on his knees* L. *of* HARDCASTLE.)

HARDCASTLE It's a pot of brass to be giving away. Get off your knees, I can't stand crawlers! Are any of your dad's relatives still alive?

BILLY Not that I know of–no!

CHARLIE I'm afraid this 'as been a shock to William. I think I'd better 'ave a conflab with me client in private. Just to discuss the legal h'aspect of the matter.

HARDCASTLE Good idea, Barnet. Piper give us a push. The pair of you must stop for t'weekend. We're having a party tonight. And by the way, we're going to dress.

(HARDCASTLE *exits hall downstage,* PIPER *pushing.*)

BILLY Be a bit chilly if we didn't.

CHARLIE Chilly! With ten thousand quid, boy, you can wrap yourself in ten pound notes.

BILLY But, Charlie, I'm not *sure* I haven't got any relations.

CHARLIE Never mind son. As long as no one turns up 'ere, we're O.K., 'cos you're the only one what can collect the money. By the way did you find your birth certificate?

BILLY Aye. (BILLY *produces it from his raincoat pocket.*)

CHARLIE (*Nodding.*) Yes. 'Cos we might need that. Now, if we're stopping for this party, I've got to find a couple of dress-suits.

BILLY And I've got to go home.

(BILLY *heads for french windows.* CHARLIE *hauls him back.*)

CHARLIE 'Ome?

BILLY I promised my missus I'd be back early.

CHARLIE You shouldn't have promised anything to that Yorkshire pudding.

BILLY My Winnie's a little beauty. (*Tapping his forehead.*) She's got it up here.

CHARLIE Just as well, she ain't got it nowhere else. You're staying 'ere till we collect the ten thousand quid. Where can I keep you out of the way for five minutes?

(CHARLIE *opens library door and* JUGG *falls in. He has two dress-suits.*)

JUGG I couldn't 'elp but h'over 'ear. I was cleanin' the key 'ole.

CHARLIE What with–you earhole?

JUGG An h'unfortunate 'abit but most useful on h'occasions. I thought these dress-suits might come in useful.

CHARLIE Marvellous! That's all we need.

JUGG May I say, Mr Barnet, I look upon this situation as most comical.

CHARLIE Yes.

JUGG Yes. I mean you passing *him* off as a portrait painter. (CHARLIE *and* JUGG *laugh.*) And passing yourself off as a solicitor. (*Both laugh.* JUGG *passes his hand out.*) And *me* passing me hand out for a fiver to keep me trap shut.

(CHARLIE *and* JUGG *choke with laughter.* BILLY *is very perplexed.* CHARLIE'S *laugh dies as he sees* JUGG'S *hand.*)

CHARLIE (*Laughing.*) That's be blackmail!

JUGG (*Laughing.*) No, no, sir – extortion.

(BILLY *bursts into laughter.*)

CHARLIE (*To* BILLY.) What are you laughing at?

BILLY I don't know.

CHARLIE You realize this is blood money.

JUGG I need the transfusion.

CHARLIE (*Going into his pocket.*) That's the last fiver you'll get.

JUGG Don't worry, it'll be well invested, sir. I've got a good tip for the dogs tonight.

(*Passing* BILLY *dinner-jacket.*) Here's your dinner-jacket.

CLIFTON (*Off.*) Has anybody seen Jugg?

CHARLIE Who's that?

JUGG Sounds like Mr Clifton Weaver. He's a critic and connoisseur of painting. (*To* BILLY.) He'll soon rumble you'er not a real artist.

BILLY Oh, 'eck! I'm off home.

(BILLY *heads out of the french windows and is replaced by double.* CHARLIE *pulls* BILLY (Double) *back by lapels of raincoat, which cover the face, into the room. N.B. The principal actor is now changing into his role of* RUPERT.)

CHARLIE Stay there and keep quiet. (*Pushing* BILLY (Double) *on to settee behind* CHARLIE *and* JUGG.) We don't want any questions asked.

DOUBLE Help!

(CHARLIE *and* JUGG *stand in front of* BILLY (Double). CLIFTON WEAVER *enters hall upstage.*)

CLIFTON Oh, Jugg, I seem to have mislaid my dinner-jacket.

JUGG (*Holding jacket behind back.*) Really, sir!

CLIFTON Yes–isn't that it?

JUGG Eh? Oh, yes, so it is. I was just knocking it–dusting it off. (*He dusts jacket.*)

CLIFTON How very kind of you. What about the trousers?

JUGG Well, what about the trousers?

CLIFTON Where are they?

JUGG I was just having them pressed. (CHARLIE *gives* JUGG *trousers which he has been sitting on.*)

CLIFTON (*Seeing trousers.*) But I can't wear them *like that*.

JUGG (*Moving them in and out, concertina fashion.*) Well, you could always *play* them like this. Now, don't worry sir, I'll have them pressed up and as good as new.

CLIFTON Thank you. (*To* CHARLIE.) Oh–I don't think we've met. My name's Weaver.

CHARLIE (*Looking at* JUGG.) We go to the same tailor.

CLIFTON Oh, really?

CHARLIE Yes–Weaver to Wearer.

(*Hand of struggling* BILLY (Double) *appears between* CHARLIE *and* JUGG.)

DOUBLE Charlie! Charlie!

CHARLIE (*Quickly.*) Charlie Barnet's the name.

CLIFTON Oh, yes, you're down here with an artist friend, Mr Hickory Wood. I'd like to see some of his work. Is he *showing anything* at the moment? (BILLY (Double) *is still struggling.*)

CHARLIE I hope not.

CLIFTON Well, maybe I'll meet him later on. Jugg–

JUGG Yes, sir?

CLIFTON Don't forget about those trousers.

(CLIFTON *exits hall downstage.*)

CHARLIE Come on, you.

(CHARLIE *pulls* (Double) *who is still on his knees, from side to settee and towards archway.*)

JUGG Downstairs.

CHARLIE (*Taking dinner-jacket.*) Take them clothes. Perform a miracle and come back looking like a gentleman.

JUGG Which constitutes a miracle.

(BILLY (Double) *rises and, with back to audience, exits hallway downstage as* RUPERT *backs on from the french windows.*)

RUPERT (*Turning.*) Oh, g-good evening.

CHARLIE Good evening.

(CHARLIE *is just about to speak to* JUGG *when he and* JUGG *react at the sight of the newcomer. They double take between* RUPERT *and one another. Finally they just stare at him in astonishment.*)

RUPERT My name's Hickory Wood. Rupert Hickory Wood.

(CHARLIE *and* JUGG *advance on him* L. RUPERT *retreats down* L.)

I've called in answer to an advertisement in the p-paper.

(CHARLIE *and* JUGG *move nearer to him down left.* RUPERT *retreats even more.*)

I-I got rather lost in the grounds and wandered through the–(*He points to the garden.*) I hope th-that's all right?

(CHARLIE *and* JUGG *move nearer.* RUPERT *retreats and looks around embarrassed and not sure what to do next.*)

It's a l-l-lovely evening.

(*Still no reaction.*)

RUPERT (*Standing by bureau.*) M–may I see Mr Hardcastle?

CHARLIE
JUGG } (*Together.*) No!

(*This makes* RUPERT *drop his case to the floor. The drawer shoots out and hits him in the behind.* CHARLIE *and* JUGG *rush over to either side of* RUPERT. CHARLIE *pulls* RUPERT'S *face and looks at it.* JUGG *does the same.*)

JUGG That face. That face–it's amazing!

CHARLIE (*Pulling* RUPERT'S *face.*) It's horrible!

RUPERT It's not that bad surely? M–may I see Mr Hardcastle?

CHARLIE / JUGG } (*Together.*) No!

CHARLIE Jugg, keep cave at the door.

JUGG Leave it to me. (JUGG *crosses to archway.*)

CHARLIE Perhaps I should have explained. I'm Charles Barnet, the legal adviser round here.

RUPERT Oh, I see.

CHARLIE Are you absolutely sure your name's Hickory Wood?

RUPERT Positive – Rupert Hickory Wood.

CHARLIE Rupert! Who was your father?

RUPERT Er – Samuel Hickory Wood.

CHARLIE How comes Billy doesn't know about you?

RUPERT Billy?

CHARLIE Yes, Billy – your twin brother.

RUPERT (*Amazed.*) My–you mean, I've got a (*rising*)– that's wonderful!

CHARLIE Marvellous! I feel sick. You mean to say you didn't know you'd got a brother.

RUPERT Well, no. You see, from what I could gather, father went broke shortly before I was born and the family had to be split up. I was brought up by a distant Auntie in Wapping.

JUGG (*In archway.*) How topping–for Wapping!

CHARLIE Well that settles that. You've come all this way for nothing. Good-bye.

(CHARLIE *starts to bustle* RUPERT *towards the french windows.*)

RUPERT But what about the advertisement in the paper. I thought I was in for some cash.

CHARLIE Well you ain't. Hardcastle is giving my Billy ten thousand quid. So long as there's no other living relative. Now you don't want to queer his pitch, do you?

RUPERT Well of course not-but–

CHARLIE So why don't you shove off?

JUGG If somebody sees him leaving now, they might think he's Mr Billy, and start asking awkward questions!

CHARLIE Oh, yes.

JUGG Why don't we *hide* him here till after the party and then he can make a surreptitious scarper.

CHARLIE Hide him, where?

JUGG I've got it, *the pantry*.

CHARLIE Somebody might find him in the pantry.

JUGG I think not, sir, me and cook have been most fortunate so far. You'll find it most congenial. I'll lay on coffee and sandwiches.

CHARLIE O.K. Off you go with JUGG.

(JUGG *holds hand out.*)

RUPERT May I take my suitcase?

CHARLIE Never mind your suitcase. And if you bump into anybody pretend you're Billy.

RUPERT How do I do that?

CHARLIE Just act stupid.

JUGG Come on.

(RUPERT *and* JUGG *exit to hall upstage.* HARDCASTLE *enters downstage of hall.*)

HARDCASTLE Barnet. Where's Hickory Wood?

CHARLIE Er – downstairs – upstairs.

HARDCASTLE He can't be in two places at once.

CHARLIE That's what you think.

HARDCASTLE Hold that, Barnet!

(*The arms on* HARDCASTLE'S *wheelchair are detachable, the right arm containing whisky and the left soda.* [Note: *On modern wheelchairs the arms are removable. The whisky is poured out of the steel tube after taking out a cork, and the soda is squirted out of the other arms by means of a rubber tube and suction ball.*] HARDCASTLE *gives* CHARLIE *his glass to hold as he helps himself to a drink.*)

HARDCASTLE (*Taking drink.*) Cheers. Now, look here, Barnet. I need a bit of help. My daughter looks as though she might make a fool of herself over this Weaver bloke. I want Billy to make sure he don't get a chance to propose to her this week-end.

CHARLIE 'Ow's 'e gonna manage that?

HARDCASTLE I don't care. See the pair of 'em are never alone. Dance every dance with Cynthia. Keep her occupied. She's coming into a lot of money one day. I don't want a bloke like Weaver to get his hands on that!

CHARLIE (*Rubbing hands gleefully.*) No!

HARDCASTLE (*Moving to door.*) You see he gets cracking. I'll tell Cynthia he's here.

CHARLIE Yes–er–what's this Miss Cynthia like?

HARDCASTLE (*Chuckling.*) That's her.

(HARDCASTLE *points to portrait down* R. *and exits to hallway downstage.* CHARLIE *turns and looks at protrait, does a double-take and removes his bowler hat.* BILLY *enters upstage from hall dressed in dress-suit and cloth cap.*)

BILLY Charlie! Charlie!

CHARLIE What's up?

BILLY I've just seen Jugg taking me downstairs.

CHARLIE Billy–that wasn't you.

BILLY Well, it was a bloke what's pinched my face.

CHARLIE He happens to be your twin brother.

BILLY I didn't know I'd got a twin brother.

CHARLIE Well, you have. But don't worry, 'e's bin taken care of. Now, 'Ardcastle wants you to do 'im a little favour.

BILLY (*Smiling.*) Oh, does 'e?

CHARLIE You've got to charm his daughter Cynthia, and keep 'er occupied.

BILLY I can't do that. My Winnie says I've got to stay celebrate.

CHARLIE Celebrate! If you succeed with Cynthia, you'll go back to your missus with a tidy sum.

BILLY With what?

CHARLIE A tidy sum.

BILLY I thought you said a tiny son.

CHARLIE And if you don't succeed with Cynthia you'll very likely get nothing.

BILLY 'Ere, what's this Cynthia look like?

CHARLIE (*Pointing to portrait.*) That's 'er.

(BILLY *looks at it and heads for french windows.*)

CHARLIE (*Hauling him back.*) Come back 'ere. You've got to make an impression on her.

BILLY Looks like someone's done it already.

CHARLIE Look Boy. If this is puttin' you off I'll turn her face to the wall.

BILLY (*Horror struck.*) Is that 'er *face*?

CHARLIE Don't worry son–she'll be gorgeous really. Gorgeous. (*He looks again.*) Oh, blimey.

BILLY Oh, well, if you say so, Charlie, I don't mind 'aving a bash.

CHARLIE 'Aving a bash! You'll have to be more subtle than that with Cynthia. She's different to your missus.

BILLY (*Looking at picture.*) Aye, she's got two noses for one thing.

CHARLIE I can see I'll have to start from the beginning with you. Now, Miss Cynthia is sitting here. (CHARLIE *indicates empty chair.*) Now as soon as you see her you go up to her and say–(*very posh*), 'Aim charmed to meet yah' go on, say it.

BILLY (*Pointing to empty chair.*) To her?

CHARLIE Yes.

BILLY (*Imitating* CHARLIE.) Aim charmed to meet you.

CHARLIE Well, act as though you're charmed. And smile when you say it.

(BILLY *leers in* CHARLIE'S *face.*)

CHARLIE Blimey, is that a smile? (BILLY *nods.*) Well, don't start laughing for Gawd's sake.

BILLY I'm sorry, Charlie.

CHARLIE You're doin' all right, son. After that you say–(*High voice.*) 'I trust I meet with your approval.'

BILLY I'll just have you on approval.

CHARLIE Meet with 'er approval.

BILLY Meet with *'er* approval.

CHARLIE Then you say 'I 'ope to get to know you better at the weekend.'

BILLY I trust I meet with your approval. I hope to get to know your weekend better. Then what do I say?

CHARLIE You'd better keep quiet after that lot.

BILLY (*To chair.*) You'd better keep quiet after that lot.

CHARLIE Just ask 'er to excuse you and go into the garden.

(BILLY *reacts to this.*)

BILLY What for?

CHARLIE Say you're going to admire the flowers.

BILLY The flowers–I can remember that.

CHARLIE Don't strain yourself. Right, you 'ang on 'ere for Miss 'Ardcastle and I'll wait out there for you in the garden. Now, put on the posh, stand up straight, look intelligent and lean nonchalantly against the chair.

(CHARLIE *indicates armchair by fireplace.* BILLY *attempts to do all at once and falls over up* C.)

BILLY I fell over.

CHARLIE (*Looking to heaven.*) Oh, Gawd!

(CHARLIE *exits through french windows.* BILLY *nervously goes to wing chair up* C. *and does his version of leaning nonchalantly.* AMY *enters from hall upstage.*)

AMY Ah, Mr Hickory Wood?

(BILLY *jumps out of his nonchalant position.*)

BILLY Aye.

AMY I'm Miss Hardcastle.

(*Pause.* BILLY *looks from* AMY *to portrait and back to* AMY.)

BILLY Oh 'eck! (*Remembering what he's been taught.*) Aim charmed to meet yah.

AMY Thank you.

BILLY Can I 'ave you on approval for the weekend?

AMY Pardon?

BILLY But you'd better keep quiet about it.

AMY Keep quiet?

BILLY Aye–I've got to go and be exused in the garden.

(BILLY *dashes out of the french windows but quickly reappears, smiling.*) Among the flowers.

(CHARLIE *pushes the reluctant* BILLY *back on.*)

BILLY Aim charmed to meet yah I'm sure.

AMY I'm Miss Hardcastle.

CHARLIE (*Sees Amy.*) Oh...

AMY Jonathan's sister.

CHARLIE 'Is sister? (*He laughs.*) There seems to have bin a slight misunderstanding. (*He raises his hat.*) Permit me–Charles Barnet.

AMY How do you do.

CHARLIE You've met Mr Hickory Wood. (BILLY *repeats* CHARLIE'S *hat business.*)

BILLY I'm charmed to meet you.

AMY Jonathan tells me he's an artist.

CHARLIE An artist? Madam you see standin' before you a veritable Leonora di Vinci. Can't you see the genius in his face–his intelligent eyes–the determined mouth? (BILLY *is endeavouring to look the role.*) Can't you see the high forehead denoting brains....

AMY (*Enthralled.*) Oh, yes I can.

CHARLIE You can?!

AMY I was wondering if Mr Hickory Wood would – grant me a small favour.

BILLY Aye, Mr Hickory Wood would, would, – I will.

CHARLIE Anything, dear lady, anything.

AMY Well, you see, my present for Cynthia hasn't arrived yet and I was wondering if Mr Hickory Wood would paint me? Just a small sketch in watercolours. I hope you don't think I'm presumptuous but it would be such a surprise for Cynthia.

CHARLIE 'Ow right you are.

BILLY But I can't paint–

CHARLIE At the moment. You see on the way down the poor boy lost 'is pallette.

BILLY Eh?

(BILLY *feels the roof of his mouth.* CHARLIE *smacks his hand.*)

CHARLIE What I mean is he's lost his painting gear.

AMY (*Rising.*) That's all right, Mr Barnet. We'll borrow Cynthia's. (*She exits into the hall downstage.*)

CHARLIE Eh? Now see what you've done. You make a mess with Cynthia, she wouldn't bother with you if you was the last man on earth.

BILLY If I was the last man on earth I'd be too busy to bother with her.

CHARLIE Ha–ha–William!

(JUGG *enters from the hallway upstage.*)

JUGG Excuse me, Mr Barnet, there's a female person inquiring for Mr Billy. She says she's his Missus! (JUGG *exits into the hall upstage.*)

BILLY Eee, it's my Winnie.

CHARLIE Winnie! What's she doing here?

BILLY I left a note for her telling her where we'd gone. (BILLY *moves to the archway.*)

CHARLIE Come back here. Since you've been down here you've told one or two minor white lies. Now, your Winnie has a nauseating regard for the truth. She'll want to know what's going on. And if I know Winnie she'll find out. And she'll talk. Now look, son, you hang on in there, I'll tell her you've gone home.

BILLY I shouldn't have secrets from my wife.

CHARLIE You shouldn't have a wife like Winnie.

(CHARLIE *pushes* BILLY *into library.* JUGG *enters from hallway upstage followed by* WINNIE.)

JUGG This way, Madam.

WINNIE Hello, Charlie.

(JUGG *coughs.*)

Thank you, my good man.

(WINNIE *tips him.*)

JUGG (*Sarcastically.*) You don't want any change, do you? (JUGG *exits hall upstage.*)

WINNIE Where's my Billy?

CHARLIE I hoped you'd ask that.

WINNIE You weren't disappointed then. Oh, Charlie Barnet, what mischief have you got him into this time?

CHARLIE Mischief? We were just down here painting the front of the house.

WINNIE So where's my Billy then?

CHARLIE Oh – he's gone home. He didn't want to work no overtime.

WINNIE I don't believe a word of it. I saw all them fancy women in the ballroom.

CHARLIE Fancy women?

WINNIE Aye, you're trying to lay my Billy on with a bit of fluff.

CHARLIE Oh, Winnie, I am not!

WINNIE Let's hope not. Anyway, he's around here somewhere. I'm not leaving 'till I find him. So there. (WINNIE *exits hall downstage.*)

CHARLIE (*Moving to hallway.*) Winnie –

(*The library door opens.* BILLY'S *head appears.*)

BILLY Can I see my Winnie?

CHARLIE No, you can't see your Winnie.

(CHARLIE *pushes* BILLY *back into library and shuts door.* CHARLIE *is moving towards archway when library door opens again and* BILLY'S (Double) *head appears.*)

BILLY (Double) Can I see my Winnie?

CHARLIE Get back in there.

(CHARLIE *again pushes* BILLY (Double) *back and closes door.* CHARLIE *exits downstage hall as* RUPERT *enters from upstage of hall.*)

RUPERT I say, Mr Barnet – could I possibly have my suitcase.

(RUPERT *crosses to his suitcase and packs it up* D.L. AMY *enters downstage of hallway with pallette and brushes.*)

AMY Oh. Mr Hickory Wood–

(RUPERT *jumps.*)

I've got the equipment. Now, how would you like me?

RUPERT I beg your pardon?

(RUPERT *looks amazed.*)

AMY (*Crossing to archway.*) I'll get the rest of the things, then you can put me where you want me.

(AMY *exits downstage of hall.* WINNIE *enters upstage of hall.*)

WINNIE (*Seeing* RUPERT.) My little luv!

(*She rushes over to* RUPERT *and jumps into his arms.* RUPERT *drops suitcase and the drawer shoots open, hitting* WINNIE'S *bottom.*)

(*Closing drawer.*) Ive been looking everywhere for you. Here, what are you doing in that dining-suite?

(RUPERT *goes to speak but* WINNIE *puts her finger to his mouth.*)

I don't want no fibs. (*Coyly.*) Don't you want to know why I've come down?

(RUPERT *opens his mouth to speak.*)

I got your note and I wanted to tell you right away. We've done it!

(*She rocks her arms.* RUPERT *looks blank.* WINNIE *rocks her arms again.* RUPERT *looks quizzical and rocks his arms.* WINNIE *points to herself then to* RUPERT *and rocks her arms.* RUPERT *points to her, then to himself, rocks his arms and stops horrified.* RUPERT *backs away.*)

Yes. After all this time. Isn't it marvellous?

RUPERT It's miraculous! I mean I couldn't, I wouldn't – I *didn't!*

(*There is a pause.*)

WINNIE Here, say that again.

RUPERT Say what again?

WINNIE What are you talking like that for?

RUPERT Like what for?

WINNIE Like the ten o'clock news.

RUPERT I think you're making a mistake–(*He rocks his arms.*)–about–er–several things.

(WINNIE *bursts into tears and sits on settee.* RUPERT *nervously edges towards hallway.* CHARLIE *enters hall upstage.*)

CHARLIE I–(*Seeing* RUPERT.) Billy or Rupert?

RUPERT Well–er–

CHARLIE Two and two?

RUPERT Four.

CHARLIE You're Rupert!

(WINNIE *rises and moves over to* CHARLIE *and* RUPERT.)

WINNIE Oh, Charlie Barnet, you're trying to turn my Billy against me.

CHARLIE You're Billy? Oh, Blimey!

RUPERT Would someone please explain–

WINNIE All this posh talk–I bet he's told those high-class girls he's single. He won't even admit he's the father of my–

(*She rocks her arms.*)

CHARLIE The father of–(CHARLIE *rocks his arms and then realizes.*) Oh, Winnie, my dear–

(CHARLIE *takes off his hat and lays it on his chest.*)

RUPERT But I'd like to say–

CHARLIE (*Quickly.*) And so would I–congratulations!

(*He shakes* RUPERT'S *hand.*)

RUPERT Now, look here, Miss–I mean Missus, I'm sure I think you're very charming. It's a great compliment and I'd like to thank you. But I certainly am not the father of your–

(*He rocks his arms and imitates a baby's cry.* WINNIE *wails.* CHARLIE *quickly puts his arm around her shoulder.*)

CHARLIE Winnie, my dear–(*Behind her back he indicates to* RUPERT *to scram whilst he takes* WINNIE *across the room.* RUPERT *exits hall upstage.*)

WINNIE (*Crying.*) I don't know what's come over him.

CHARLIE It's a bit of a shock 'aving a baby.

WINNIE But why's he gone all lah-de-dah? He used to be so sweet and now he's proper daft.

(*She wails.* BILLY *enters from library.*)

BILLY Winnie, luv, what's the matter–what you crying for?

WINNIE Oh, you've dropped it now, have you?

BILLY (*Looking around.*) Dropped what?

WINNIE (*Tearfully.*) And I thought you'd be that pleased about–you know.

(WINNIE *rocks her arms.*)

BILLY Eh?

CHARLIE You know!

(CHARLIE *rocks his arms.* BILLY *repeats it.*)

BILLY (*Realizing.*) You mean–?

(CHARLIE *nods.*)

I'm a daddy!

(*He collapses into armchair down* R.)

WINNIE Are you all right, luv. Take it easy.

BILLY (*Stirring*.) Winnie, my little luv!

WINNIE You didn't seem all that pleased the first time.

BILLY Do you mean this is the second one we've had?

WINNIE Come on, luv, let's go home.

CHARLIE No! He's stopping 'ere. *You* go home and rest.

BILLY Aye. Charlie says I've got to keep Cynthia busy.

WINNIE Cynthia busy?

BILLY It's all right, I'll be home as soon as I've left an impression on her.

WINNIE I thought you were up here after fancy women. Well don't fret. I'm going to find this Cynthia and sort her out. (WINNIE *exits hall downstage.*)

BILLY Oh, Charlie, we won't 'alf cop it now.

CHARLIE Go after 'er and keep 'er occupied.

BILLY 'Ow?

CHARLIE Oh. Tell 'er she's a little luv.

BILLY Oh, aye. (*Rushing out into hallway.*) Winnie, you are a little luv!

(BILLY *exits hall downstage.* JUGG *appears from behind archway curtain upstage.*)

JUGG Things are very tricky, Mr Barnet, very tricky indeed.

CHARLIE You're a great comfort you are. There must be an easier way of earnin' ten thousand quid.

JUGG Why don't you try *bingo?*

CHARLIE 'Ere, can you fix me up with another dress-suit?

JUGG I'll try a different outfitter. Drop. (JUGG *holds hand out.*)

CHARLIE Can't I have this one on tick.

JUGG Certainly not, terms strictly cash. That reminds me, you owe me a quid for Mr Rupert's sandwiches.

CHARLIE (*Taking out wallet.*) A pound? What was in 'em–ten bob notes?

JUGG No, sir–dripping.

(JUGG *takes pound note and exits library.* RUPERT *enters stealthily from hall upstage.*)

CHARLIE Billy or Rupert?–two and two?

RUPERT Four.

CHARLIE Rupert. (*Realizing.*) What are you doing back in 'ere?

RUPERT Trying to get my suitcase.

CHARLIE Never mind your perishin' suitcase. Push off to the pantry.

CYNTHIA (*Off.*) In here, daddy?

(CHARLIE *pushes* RUPERT *behind him.* CYNTHIA *enters from hall downstage.*)

CYNTHIA (*To* CHARLIE.) Good evening. Mr Hickory Wood?

CHARLIE No!

CYNTHIA Daddy said I'd find him here and I was to introduce myself. I'm Cynthia Hardcastle.

(RUPERT *has 'popped' his head over* CHARLIE'S *shoulder. He is immediately taken with her.*)

RUPERT Are you really?

CYNTHIA (*Laughing.*) Mr Hickory Wood?

RUPERT Yes, thank you very much.

CYNTHIA How do you do?

RUPERT I do very well, thank you.

(*They look at each other*.)

CHARLIE I'm Charles Barnet. (*No one takes any notice of him.*)...I'm Charles Barnet.

RUPERT (*Turns and shakes hands.*) How do you do? Oh! (*To* CYNTHIA.) This is Mr Barnet–Billy's adviser, I mean *my* adviser.

CYNTHIA How do you do.

(RUPERT *and* CYNTHIA *are still shaking hands.*)

RUPERT How, how, how do you do.

(*Pause while they still shake hands*.)

CHARLIE Have you struck oil, yet?

CYNTHIA Mr Hickory Wood. Drinks are being served by the swimming pool.

CHARLIE You'll catch your death of cold out there.

CYNTHIA That's all right–I'll get my wrap.

CHARLIE Good idea. Don't 'urry. Mr Hickory Wood will be 'ere when you get back. (CYNTHIA *exits into hallway downstage.*) ...but not this one. (*To* RUPERT.) Downstairs you.

RUPERT I say, she's rather nice isn't she?

(CHARLIE *pushes* RUPERT *towards hall as* AUNT AMY *enters from hall downstage.* CHARLIE *rushes* RUPERT *towards french windows.* AMY *carries a large canvas.*)

AMY Ah, Mr. Hickory Wood–are you ready for me?

RUPERT P-pardon?

AMY — I've got the rest of Cynthia's things.

RUPERT — What on earth does she want me to do?

CHARLIE — Paint her.

RUPERT — Paint–b-but I only dabble.

CHARLIE — Get dabbling. You can do better than Billy can.

RUPERT — Billycan?

(RUPERT *laughs*.)

AMY — I'll get the easel. (*Seeing it behind the screen.*) Oh! There it is–Oh, that Jugg! Oh, Billy, would you get the easel. Billy?

CHARLIE — (*Kneeing him.*) That's you.

RUPERT — Oh, yes, a pleasure.

(RUPERT *crosses to behind screen and is replaced by* (Double).)

CHARLIE — If you'd sit there, Modom.

(CHARLIE *sits* AMY *on round settee facing front.* RUPERT (Double) *backs on–carrying easel and sets it up* C. BILLY *rushes in from study.*)

BILLY — Charlie, Charlie, I can't find my Winnie anywhere.

(CHARLIE *moves towards* BILLY *then grabs* RUPERT (Double) *by collar and trousers and propels him out of french windows.*)

AMY — (*Turning.*) Who was that?

CHARLIE — Jugg – going for an even' stroll. Right, William – put the canvas up.

BILLY — We goin' sailing?

CHARLIE — Ha, ha. No, you're goin' paintin'. Put the board on the easel. (*The horrified* BILLY *does so.*)

BILLY (*To* CHARLIE.) What do I do first?

CHARLIE First put 'er where you want to paint 'er.

(BILLY *doing his best to imitate an artist, keeps re-posing* AMY *until finally she is staring up at the ceiling with her arms outstretched.*)

~~BILLY~~ Charlie What's she doing–directing the traffic?

CHARLIE (*To* BILLY.) Wrap it up!

(BILLY *wraps* AMY'S *lace stole round her head.*)

Are you gonna paint 'er with mumps? (*He crosses to her.*) I beg you pardon, Modom–Modom? Now she's gone deaf. Just as well.

BILLY What do I do now?

CHARLIE Stand back, son, and I'll show you. You take the brush–so. You dip it in the pallet so. Shake of the superflousity – and you're in business.

(CHARLIE *walks mincingly, dips an imaginary paint brush in oil, flicks and poses.* BILLY *copies him. He dips a real paint brush in the paint and flicks it in* CHARLIE'S *face.* BILLY *smiles at him. Then seeing the paint on* CHARLIE'S *face, gives him a moustache and sideburns.*)

CHARLIE (*Sweetly.*) You've forgotten the beard.

(BILLY *gives him a beard.* CHARLIE *takes cloth and wipes his face.*)

BILLY Now what?

(CHARLIE *holds his arm out with his thumb pointing upwards.*)

CHARLIE (*Demonstrating.*) Thumb. Thumb–perspective. Thumb–perspective!

BILLY Thump 'er what?

CHARLIE Get the perspective of 'er face with your thumb–now paint it.

(BILLY *paints his thumb.*)

CHARLIE 'Er face!

(BILLY *advances on* AMY *with a brush.*)

CHARLIE Come back 'ere! Oh, blimey–'ere I'll give you a start.

(CHARLIE *paints an oval. Denoting outline of a face.*)

Fill that in.

(BILLY, *taking* CHARLIE *at his word completely fills it in with black paint.*)

CHARLIE The only living artist who can paint a hole.

(CHARLIE *turns canvas to the other side and paints another oval face.*)

That at the bottom is her chin.

[Note: *See diagram of completed drawing on page 134.*]

CHARLIE Start with 'er eyes–as if she were gazing up.

(BILLY *paints two crossed eyes at the top of the face. He adds long eyelashes.*)

Looks like two fleas in a bucket.

(BILLY *fills the eyes in with red paint.*)

What's the red for?

BILLY She's been on the booze.

CHARLIE All right put her hair on.

(BILLY *paints three hairs on top of the head.*)

You've forgotten the bails!

(BILLY *adds bails.*)

CHARLIE What about her ear? (*Shouting.*) Where's her ear?!

BILLY She's sitting on it!

CHARLIE 'Er ear 'ere–not 'er ear there!

(BILLY *paints a big ear down the left side of her face and then adds an earring in the shape of a pawnbroker's sign with three balls.*)

Don't do another one son, you'll make 'er top heavy. Better do her mouth next.

(BILLY *paints a small mouth.*)

BILLY She's whistling.

CHARLIE What about 'er teeth?

BILLY She blew em out.

CHARLIE Now, do 'er nose.

(BILLY *paints a red nose sticking out from the right side of the face. He adds nose drops.* CHARLIE *catches the final one in his hat.*)

'Er nose goes 'ere.

(CHARLIE *draws two perpendicular lines in the middle of the face.* BILLY *crosses them with two horizontal lines and puts a cross in top corner. Before* CHARLIE *realizes he's inviegled into a game of noughts and crosses.* BILLY *wins.*)

CHARLIE (*Turning to* AMY.) Modom, this is going to 'urt you more than it 'urts me.

AMY It is finished?

BILLY (*Proudly.*) Aye.

(AMY *crosses and looks at portrait. She screams and faints into* BILLY'S *arms.* WINNIE *enters from hall downstage.*)

WINNIE Ah! I thought you were after fancy women.

BILLY But, Winnie, love....

(BILLY *quickly passes* AMY *over to* CHARLIE, WINNIE *chases* BILLY *across room.* BILLY *trips and gets his head stuck in the gramophone horn. The horn comes off the gramophone and* BILLY *staggers backwards towards the french windows.*)

CURTAIN

ACT TWO

The action is continuous. BILLY, (Double) *the horn still on his head, staggers out of french windows.*

WINNIE Billy! Billy!

CHARLIE It's all a mistake, Winnie.

WINNIE I'll deal with you later, Charlie Barnet. (*To* AMY.) And as for you – you should be ashamed of yourself – fast cat. BILLY! Billy!

(Winnie *runs out of french windows after* BILLY, *followed by* CHARLIE. HARDCASTLE *and* PIPER, *with briefcase, enter from hall upstage*).

HARDCASTLE Why aren't you lot in t' ballroom. (*Seeing portrait.*) What the 'eck's that?

AMY It's Mr. Hickory Wood's portrait of me, Jonathan.

HARDCASTLE Portrait of you, Amy? Oh, I see what he's getting at. Aye.

PIPER I think we ought to sue him for defamation of character.

(*A Waltz is heard playing the ballroom.*)

AMY I'll get Jugg to frame it.

PIPER Allow me. Miss Amy, they're playing a waltz, would you care to join me?

AMY Oh, thank you, Mr Piper.

(PIPER *takes portrait down from the easel.*)

HARDCASTLE Piper, don't you let that bag out of your sight.

(PIPER *looks at* AMY.)

PIPER Mr Hardcastle!

HARDCASTLE (*Pointing to the briefcase.*) *That* bag.

PIPER Oh.

(PIPER *and* AMY *exit into the hall upstage.* HARDCASTLE *takes a quick look to see if the coast is clear then unscrews the knob of his walking stick. He pours a drink out of the stick into knob and drinks.*)

HARDCASTLE Jugg!

(JUGG *enters from library.*)

JUGG Always on the alert, sir.

HARDCASTLE Jugg, get me a refill.

JUGG Yes, with pleasure, sir. Brandy, sir?

HARDCASTLE Aye. And get that damned easel out of here.

JUGG (*Taking easel.*) That also will be a pleasure, 'pop goes the easel'.

(JUGG *exits hall downstage with easel.* CHARLIE *enters french windows.*)

HARDCASTLE Is Billy keeping my Cynthia occupied?

CHARLIE Oh yus, Mr H.

HARDCASTLE Good, I'll go and meet the rest of the guests. Be too bad for you if some more Hickory Woods arrive with 'em.

CHARLIE Don't say that, not even in jest.

(HARDCASTLE *exits into hall upstage laughing.* RUPERT *enters from french windows.*)

RUPERT I say –

CHARLIE Oh – two and two?

RUPERT Four.

CHARLIE Rupert, what are you doing back here?

RUPERT It's getting chilly out there.

CHARLIE Why don't you get back to the pantry.

(CYNTHIA *enters from hall downstage with wrap.*)

RUPERT Oh. I say.

CYNTHIA Have I kept you waiting?

RUPERT Of course not.

CYNTHIA Now what about our drink in the garden.

CHARLIE *No,* you can't you take him into the garden.

CYNTHIA Why not?

CHARLIE Look what 'appened to Adam and Eve.

(CYNTHIA *laughs.*)

CYNTHIA (*Offering arm.*) Billy?

RUPERT (*Dreamily.*) I wish I was. I'm glad I am.

(RUPERT *goes to follow and* CHARLIE *trips him up. As* CYNTHIA *turns* RUPERT *flies into her arms and both fall on to settee.* WINNIE *enters from french windows.*)

WINNIE Oh! You're at it again are you? I've been looing for you in t' garden. And where's that thing you were wearing on your head?

CHARLIE Now look here, Winnie –

WINNIE Keep quiet. That girl – that girl was cuddling you.

RUPERT Was she?

WINNIE Well, what about me?

RUPERT I don't think she'd want to cuddle you.

CYNTHIA May I ask what you're doing here?

WINNIE Getting my Billy out of it.

RUPERT Your Billy? Oh, I see – this belongs to Billy.

(*He rocks his arms.*)

WINNIE Oh, so you admit it now, do you.

RUPERT Yes – no!

CYNTHIA Look, I think you're making a mistake.

(WINNIE *crosses to* CYNTHIA)

WINNIE: You keep out of this. You're no better than you ought to be.

(BILLY (Double) *enters from french windows with horn on head.* RUPERT *is standing near cabinet door.* CHARLIE *quickly pushes* RUPERT *into cabinet and shuts door.*)

CYNTHIA: I think you're mad.

WINNIE: Aye, good and mad. Inviting my Billy down here to paint your front and them making eyes at him round the back.

BILLY (Double): Help!

(*They turn and see* BILLY (Double) *in horn.*)

CYNTHIA: What on earth – ?

WINNIE: What's he doing back in that thing?

CYNTHIA: He'll suffocate in there.

CHARLIE: (*Lifting* BILLY *up.*) I'll take him along to the kitchen and get a tin opener.

(*Muffled sounds from horn.* HARDCASTLE *enters from hall upstage.*)

HARDCASTLE: What's all the rumpus about? (*Seeing* BILLY.) Who's that?

CHARLIE: It's Billy, Mr H.

(BILLY (Double) *is staggering about.*)

HARDCASTLE: Billy. What's he doing?

CHARLIE: Sailor's hornpipe.

HARDCASTLE: Silly young fool. (*Tapping horn.*) Come out.

BILLY (Double): (*Voice muffled.*) What's that?

WINNIE: (*Shouting into horn.*) Billy!

(BILLY (Double) *jerks backwards and forwards C. stage.*)

CYNTHIA Will you please be quiet.

HARDCASTLE (*Getting angry.*) Will you lot shut-up! (*Moving to table.*) Young lady, would you come over here, and you, Cynthia. Now see here, miss. . . .

WINNIE Missus, if you don't mind.

(CYNTHIA *and* WINNIE *move over to table as* RUPERT *tiptoes out of cabinet.* CHARLIE *has dashed over to french windows and pushed* BILLY (Double) *down beside chest and stands in front of him.*)

CHARLIE (*To* RUPERT.) Quick, the garden.

RUPERT P-pardon?

CHARLIE G-garden.

HARDCASTLE (*Turns and Sees* RUPERT.) Oh, you're out of that contraption, are you?

RUPERT What contraption?

HARDCASTLE The gramophone horn, you were wearing on your nut! Remember?

RUPERT Oh! Oh, yes. (*Laughing.*) I don't think it suited me. I – I take it you're Mr Hardcastle.

HARDCASTLE Of course I'm Mr Hardcastle.

RUPERT I'm very pleased to meet you.

HARDCASTLE What the blazes are you talking about. And where did you get this lad-de-dah voice from?

(BILLY (Double) *starts to rise and* CHARLIE *quickly sits* RUPERT *on horn.*)

RUPERT (*Being pushed up and down by the struggling* BILLY (Double).) Lah-de-dah-di?

CHARLIE (*Quickly.*) I'm very glad you asked that Mr H. It was during the war. 'E was at 'Arrow at the time and they evacuated him to the University at 'Alifax.

RUPERT Yes, that's quite right – Halifax! (*He shoots up.*)

HARDCASTLE What're you bobbing up and down for?

RUPERT It – er – must be the beans I had for lunch.

HARDCASTLE Beans?

RUPERT Yes – jumping beans!

HARDCASTLE I don't know what's the matter with everybody. Come over here, Barnet.

CHARLIE (*Aside to* RUPERT – *pointing to* BILLY.) Get rid of 'im.

(RUPERT *attempts to get* BILLY (Double) – *the horn on his head – out of french windows.*)

HARDCASTLE Young lady, will you tell me what you're doing in my house?

WINNIE I'm getting my Billy out of it.

CYNTHIA He says he doesn't even know you.

WINNIE He's my husband.

(RUPERT, *in his effort to get* BILLY (Double) *out of french windows, blows down the horn, which makes a fog horn sound and propels* BILLY *into garden.*)

HARDCASTLE (*Turning.*) Now what are your doing?

RUPERT Bird watching.

HARDCASTLE What was that noise?

RUPERT The mating call.

HARDCASTLE This is serious – this young lady says she's married to you.

WINNIE Yes.

RUPERT No she is not.

WINNIE What?

CYNTHIA (*To* RUPERT.) Are you sure?

RUPERT I'm positive – she's married – er – to Mr Barnet. (*Points to* CHARLIE.)

CHARLIE Eh?

WINNIE What!

CYNTHIA Well, why didn't you say so?

CHARLIE (*Coyly.*) Well – We was trying to keep it a secret.

(WINNIE *bursts into tears.*)

There, there, Winnie, my love don't get excited. (*He takes her in his arms and covers her face. He threatens* RUPERT. RUPERT *smiles.*)

HARDCASTLE Your Missus seems a bit overwrought, you and her had better stop for the weekend.

CHARLIE Yes – Eh!

HARDCASTLE Then you'll be able to keep an eye on her.

CHARLIE Oh. Yes, there is that.

(WINNIE *wails.*)

P'haps you'd better stay, Winnie, my little love.

WINNIE I don't know what you're up to, Charlie Barnet. (*To* RUPERT.) Are we stopping then?

RUPERT Oh, yes, rather.

(AMY *enters from hall upstage with a cardboard box. Crosses to* HARDCASTLE *down R.*)

AMY Jonathan, you promised to pick the winning raffle ticket.

HARDCASTLE Oh aye. Amy, this young lady's stopping for the weekend. She's Mr Barnet's Missus.

WINNIE I'm Billy's Missus. (*She flings her arms round* RUPERT.) Aren't I Billy?

HARDCASTLE (*To* AMY.) She's a bit upset at the moment. Mr. Barnet's very good with her.

AMY Oh, poor girl. (*To* WINNIE.) Anyway, we're having a party tonight. You'll enjoy that.

WINNIE I haven't got me party frock.

CYNTHIA Never mind. You can borrow one of mine. Come along.

HARDCASTLE (*Laughing.*) Aye, we're having dancing and all, you and Mr Barnet can have a second honeymoon. (WINNIE *lets out a wail as* CYNTHIA *and she exit hall downstage.* AMY *and* HARDCASTLE *are by the table selecting raffle tickets.* BILLY (Double) *enters from french windows, the horn still on his head.* CHARLIE *and* RUPERT *make a grab for him but miss.* CHARLIE *opens the cocktail cabinet door and quickly pushes the protesting* RUPERT *inside.*)

[NOTE. *During the following dialogue the principal actor and Double change places as follows:* BILLY (Double), *the horn on his head, falls behind armchair back while* BILLY (Double), *unseen by audience, takes his head out of horn and crawls behind* HARDCASTLE, AMY *and downstage right table. He leaves the stage by means of concealed flap in the wall between library door and downstage table. The principal actor then enters by same methods and gets into horn.* *See diagram on Page 133.*]

HARDCASTLE (*Turning.*) What the –

CHARLIE 'E's done it again. Silly boy.

AMY Is that Mr Hickory Wood in there?

CHARLIE Yus, it's 's deaf aid.

AMY It's very large.

CHARLIE Well 'e's very deaf.

HARDCASTLE He's not deaf at all! He's playing the fool again.

AMY Surely, it's part of my gramophone.

CHARLIE 'E's very musical.

AMY How on earth did he get in there?

CHARLIE Oh 'e's always popping in and out.

HARDCASTLE Get him out of it.

(CHARLIE *struggles to get horn off* BILLY'S *head which he replaces on gramophone.*).

BILLY I staggered all round t'garden.

HARDCASTLE You haven't left the room.

BILLY Well if I haven't left the room. You must have a lot of trees in here.

(CYNTHIA *enters from hall downstage.*)

CYNTHIA I've lent Mrs Barnet a dress.

HARDCASTLE Well, fix the rest of us up with straight jackets. We're all going round t' bend. I'm going to have a drink.

(HARDCASTLE *moves to cocktail cabinet.*)

CHARLIE (*Aghast.*) No!

HARDCASTLE What do you mean – no?

CHARLIE You mustn't drink – you're drivin'. (*He pushes* HARDCASTLE *away.*) Billy, get Mr H. a brandy.

(BILLY *opens cabinet door and* RUPERT'S (Double) *hand passes out brandy.* BILLY *takes it, reacts, screams and flees out of french windows.*)

HARDCASTLE Barnet, where's he gone with my brandy?

CHARLIE For the soda.

HARDCASTLE The soda. Where from?

CHARLIE From the fountain. I'll get him.

(CHARLIE *goes out into garden.*)

AMY — Mr Hickory Wood's, behaving very strangely, Jonathan. Do you think he drinks?

CYNTHIA — I shouldn't think so. I expect he's excited about the money.

(*Cocktail cabinet opens and* RUPERT *stealthily tiptoes towards french windows.*)

HARDCASTLE — (*Turning.*) Oh, you're back are you?

RUPERT — (*Jumping.*) Am I? Oh, yes. It was getting – stuffy.

HARDCASTLE — In the garden?

RUPERT — Is that where I've been?

HARDCASTLE — What have you done with my brandy?

RUPERT — I never touch the stuff.

HARDCASTLE — You just rushed out into the garden with it.

RUPERT — What did I do that for?

HARDCASTLE — Well, I don't know. Go and get my brandy back – and Barnet too.

RUPERT — Yes – where is he?

HARDCASTLE — He was with you, wasn't he?

RUPERT — (*Opening cabinet.*) I don't think so. No.

HARDCASTLE — In the garden!

RUPERT — Oh, yes. (*To* CYNTHIA.) I'm sorry I've been behaving a little strangely.

CYNTHIA — That's all right. Hurry back and we'll join the party.

RUPERT — I'd like that–I'll go and get Mr Brandy and a bottle of Barnet. (*He dithers out of french windows.*)

AMY I don't know if it's my imagination but I thought Mr Hickory Wood spoke with a North Country accent.

CYNTHIA Did you – well I expect he's trying to improve his speech but sometimes forgets.

HARDCASTLE Well I don't know.

CYNTHIA I must say he does seem a little absent minded.

AMY (*Knowingly.*) But quite nice looking, dear.

(CHARLIE *and* BILLY *enter from french windows.* BILLY *holds the brandy bottle.*)

BILLY 'Ere, you didn't give me a chance to say 'ullo.

HARDCASTLE 'Ullo to who?

BILLY My brother.

CHARLIE (*Quickly.*) Jugg.

HARDCASTLE Jugg. What's he doing in the garden?

CHARLIE Planting berries.

HARDCASTLE It's pitch black.

BILLY Aye, they're blackberries.

(WINNIE *enters from hall downstage in white evening dress.*)

BILLY Oh, Winnie love.

WINNIE What do you think of the dress, Billy?

BILLY You look like a cream horn.

WINNIE The band's playing.

CYNTHIA Would you like to dance, Billy?

BILLY Aye, come on, Winnie.

(WINNIE *smiles at* CYNTHIA *and drags him off, upstage of hall.*)

CYNTHIA Well really! I'd better give Clifton the dance I promised him.

AMY Now don't worry, Cynthia, dear.

(AMY *and* CYNTHIA *exit into hall upstage.*)

HARDCASTLE Barnet, Billy shouldn't be gallivanting about with your missus.

CHARLIE You're so right, Mr H.

HARDCASTLE Well, tell him to get cracking with Cynthia on the dance floor. 'E can dance can't 'e?

CHARLIE He ain't called twinkle-toes for nothing.

HARDCASTLE I'll tell Cynthia he's panting for the next dance. I might have a go myself – musical chairs.

(HARDCASTLE *exits upstage of the hall.* CHARLIE *moves to french windows.* WEAVER *enters from the library.*)

CLIFTON Ah! Mr Barnet. I was looking for Cynthia. She promised me the next dance.

CHARLIE Bad luck son. My Billy's booked it. And all the others.

CLIFTON Your Billy's becoming rather a thorn in my side, Mr Barnet, I have my own plans for Cynthia.

CHARLIE I bet you have.

CLIFTON And they do not include Mr Hickory Wood. I'd be most upset if I thought he was – er – poaching on my preserves.

CHARLIE Well, may the best man win.

CLIFTON I'm sure I will. I've spent a considerable amount of time – and money – cultivating Cynthia. I do not intend to come away empty handed (*Smiling and flicking his cigarette-ash into* CHARLIE'S *bowler hat.*) I trust you see my point.

(CHARLIE *replaces his hat and sneezes as the ash falls out of hat.* WEAVER *exits hall downstage.* JUGG *enters from upstage of hall.*)

JUGG Trouble, Mr Barnet. Big trouble.

CHARLIE What's up.

JUGG It's that Winnie. She's creating in the ballroom trying to find out from Mr Billy what's going on.

CHARLIE Oh Gawd! We'll 'ave to get Winnie out of Billy's way.

JUGG I've a much better idea. Let's get Winnie out of *everybody's* way.

CHARLIE 'Ow we gonna manage that?

JUGG (*Taking box from pocket.*) Sleepin' pills.

CHARLIE (*Shocked.*) Sleepin' pills? (*Hopefully.*) Are they 'armful?

JUGG On the contrary – they're very beneficial. She'll wake up after a couple of hours feeling most refreshed.

CHARLIE Marvelous, she needs a little rest, anyway.

JUGG I'll pass it off as the punch being too potent.

CHARLIE Jugg, Jugg, you're worth your weight in gold.

JUGG I will be when I've finished with you. (*He holds out his hand.* CHARLIE *stops laughing and forks out.*) And now to pep up the punch post haste.

(JUGG *exits hall upstage.* RUPERT *comes in from french windows.*)

RUPERT I say.

CHARLIE Billy or Rupert?

RUPERT Well – er – two and two?

CHARLIE Four.

RUPERT I'm Rupert. I've been looking for you and a bottle of brandy.

CHARLIE Never mind the drink son. I've got a little idea for you.

RUPERT I'm not too keen on your ideas.

CHARLIE Now look – Billy's supposed to be impressing Cynthia and keeping her occupied. I think Cynthia's more likely to be impressed with your charm and manners than what she is with Billy's.

RUPERT Thank you.

CHARLIE Not only that, Weaver's turning nasty. You'll be able to deal with him better than Billy, so we'll keep Billy out of the way while you get cracking on Cynthia.

RUPERT Oh, that's a good idea.

CHARLIE As Billy – on the dance floor.

RUPERT That's not such a good idea. I don't dance very well.

CHARLIE Good – Eh? You've only got to keep time with the band.

RUPERT I do, but they won't keep time with me. Honestly, Mr Barnet, my left foot doesn't know what my right foot's doing.

CHARLIE Billy's left foot doesn't even know it's got a right foot.

(CYNTHIA *enters from hall upstage.*)

CYNTHIA Oh, Billy. Daddy tells me you'd like to dance.

RUPERT Is it an excuse me?

CYNTHIA I expect so.

RUPERT Good – excuse me.

CHARLIE Oh, he's so shy. He doesn't like dancing with all these people around.

CYNTHIA (*Laughing.*) I see. That's all right we'll play the gramophone in here.

(CYNTHIA *laughs and goes to select a record.*)

RUPERT (*To* CHARLIE.) Honestly, Mr Barnet, I'd better go.

CYNTHIA Go?

(*The music starts.*)

RUPERT Oh, I'm – going for a jiffy, won't be a glass of water. I need a drink.

(RUPERT *exits hall downstage.* CYNTHIA *goes to change the record.*)

CHARLIE (*Calling after him.*) Come back limping and say you've sprained your ankle. (*The music stops.*) Come back limping. . .(*To* CYNTHIA.) Gone quiet, ain't it? Ain't that lad just busting' with charm and H'elegance?

CYNTHIA (*Laughing.*) Yes – he's certainly different.

(BILLY *enters from upstage of hall.*)

BILLY It's a champion party.

CHARLIE Scarper, Rupert's taken over from you.

CYNTHIA (*Turning.*) Oh, you weren't thirsty.

BILLY Eh?

CHARLIE The water was too cold – limp?

BILLY What for?

CHARLIE Limp! (*He stamps his foot.*)

BILLY Ouch!

CHARLIE Oh dear, now 'e's sprained his ankle.

BILLY No I 'aven't. You trod on me foot.

CHARLIE Anyway, you can't dance now – what a shame.

(The record starts to play the tango 'Jealousy'.)

BILLY No, I'm all right. 'Eee that's nice music. What sort of a dance do you do to that?

CHARLIE You can't even walk straight let alone dance.

CYNTHIA (*Adjusting gramophone.*) It's a tango.

BILLY I've seen it on the 'telly' – I'm all right once I get going.

CHARLIE Get goin' out of the door.

CYNTHIA Ready, Billy?

BILLY Aye.

(BILLY *sticks his bottom out and approaches* CYNTHIA *with arms outstretched.*)

CHARLIE No! Don't do it, son.

BILLY 'Ere, this is the dance where you waggle your bottom.

CHARLIE Oh, Gawd! (CHARLIE *sinks into a chair down* R. *and holds his head.* BILLY *and* CYNTHIA *go into a comedy tango. At one point the record gets stuck.* BILLY *stamps on the floor, the 'trick' drawer shoots open and propels them across the stage.* CYNTHIA *falls into chair exhausted. For the want of a partner,* BILLY *grabs* CHARLIE *who ends up crawling on the floor.* BILLY *takes this as a cue to go into a bullfighting routing. With a rose between his teeth and the red shawl, he makes 'passes' at the crawling* CHARLIE. BILLY *then drops the shawl over* CHARLIE'S *head, grabs a sword from the wall, plunges it between* CHARLIE'S *legs with an 'Olez', leaps out of the french windows.*)

CHARLIE 'E's gone into the garden. Perhaps I'd better go after him, before he breaks into a floral dance. I'll kill him.

(CHARLIE *rushes out of the french windows into the garden.* CYNTHIA *laughing, crosses to stop record and closes bureau drawer.* CLIFTON *comes in from hall downstage.*)

CLIFTON Ah, there you are, Cynthia.

CYNTHIA (*Far away.*) Um?

CLIFTON I've been looking everywhere for you, my dear.

CYNTHIA Have you?

CLIFTON Yes, I haven't seen you all evening.

CYNTHIA I've been dancing with Mr Hickory Wood.

CLIFTON Oh?

CYNTHIA Yes, he's quite fantastic.

CLIFTON You seem to be spending a lot of time with him. (*Moving to her.*) Don't forget I'm your guest too.

(CLIFTON *moves closer to her.*)

CYNTHIA (*Moving.*) Now, Clifton –

CLIFTON I see. This Hickory Wood seems to have affected you somewhat.

CYNTHIA Oh really, I hardly know him.

CLIFTON (*Smirking.*) Love at first sight?

CYNTHIA (*Sitting on the settee.*) Don't be silly.

CLIFTON It's you who's silly, my dear. He's not half good enough for you.

CYNTHIA Isn't he?

CLIFTON What can he offer you? No position – no money.

(CHARLIE *enters from the french windows.*)

CYNTHIA (*Moving away.*) Perhaps those things don't interest me.

CLIFTON (*Going close.*) My dear, Cynthia, I can read you like a book.

CHARLIE (*Standing behind them.*) Well, stop thumbing over the pages. Not intrudin' I 'ope?

CYNTHIA No, I believe Mr. Weaver was just leaving.

CLIFTON (*Crossing to the hall.*) Very well, perhaps you'll give me one dance tonight.

CYNTHIA (*Coyly.*) Oh, yes – I think I might manage that.

(WEAVER *reacts and exits hall upstage.*)

CHARLIE You know, Miss Cynthia, I don't care for that fellow.

CYNTHIA Perhaps he's not your type, Mr Barnet.

CHARLIE What I mean is – you can't compare him with the h'elegant and charming Billy. Can you?

CYNTHIA No. I must admit Mr Hickory Wood is different.

CHARLIE Oh, yes. He is.

CYNTHIA In fact, he seems different every time I meet him.

CHARLIE (*Meaningly.*) Yes.

(JUGG *enters from hall downstage with dress-suit.*)

JUGG Mr B. I thought you might like to know that I've dealt with Winnie.

CYNTHIA Oh, what's that, Jugg?

JUGG I've been attending to Mrs Barnet's sleepin' h'arrangements.

CYNTHIA Oh, good, have you fixed her up?

JUGG (*Nodding.*) Oh, yes.

(RUPERT *enters from hall downstage with exaggerated limp crossing to* C.)

RUPERT I say, Cynthia, I seem to have hurt my ankle . . .

CHARLIE Never mind!

CYNTHIA You were quite marvellous.

RUPERT Was I?

CYNTHIA Show me those steps again.

RUPERT What steps?

CHARLIE The steps into the garden, I'm sure you must be very thirsty.

CYNTHIA Yes. I know, we'll go down to the pool and have a long drink.

RUPERT I'm not as thirsty as all that.

(RUPERT *and* CYNTHIA *exit through the french windows.*)

CHARLIE In 'is hands rests my future.

JUGG *Our* future. Here's your dinner-jacket.

CHARLIE Ta. There ain't gonna be no repercussions this time are there?

JUGG Oh, no, sir. I *borrowed* them from the second drummer.

CHARLIE Eh?

JUGG It's all right 'E can always hide behind his triangle.

(JUGG *exits into library.* BILLY *dashes in hall upstage.*)

BILLY Charlie! Charlie!

CHARLIE What's up?

BILLY It's my Winnie. I don't like the look of her.

CHARLIE Well that makes two of us.

BILLY She took one swig of punch and just passed out.

CHARLIE Don't worry she always had a weak head. I'll see she comes to no harm. Now you keep out of the way while Rupert does the rest.

(CHARLIE *pushes* BILLY *towards library.*)

BILLY There's nowt to do in there.

CHARLIE Read this.

BILLY What is it?

CHARLIE Telephone Directory.

(CHARLIE *gives him the telephone directory from table up* C. *and pushes him into library.* PIPER *enters hall upstage pushing* HARDCASTLE.)

HARDCASTLE (*To* CHARLIE.) Barnet! Barnet. Your Billy must be doing a good job, Barnet. That Weaver's not doing so well with our Cynthia.

CHARLIE He's a good lad is my Billy.

HARDCASTLE Might as well get the agreement signed. I can't see no other Hickory Woods turning up.

CHARLIE Thank Gawd for that.

HARDCASTLE Piper are you still clutching that briefcase Piper?

PIPER Oh, yes, Mr Hardcastle.

(PIPER *produces* AMY'S *knitting bag.*)

HARDCASTLE That's Amy's knitting bag.

PIPER Oh, dear!

HARDCASTLE You blithering idiot! There's ten thousand pounds in that briefcase.

PIPER I had it when I was dancing with Miss Amy. We must have got mixed up.

HARDCASTLE Well push up back into the ballroom. If you've lost that money, Piper, I'll make you marry Amy first thing int' morning.

PIPER Oh, Mr Hardcastle.

HARDCASTLE And I'll spread round a rumour what the hurry was.

(PIPER *and* HARDCASTLE *exit into hall upstage.* JUGG *enters from library laughing.*)

CHARLIE What are you laughing at?

JUGG Well it struck me as being rather comical, after all the money you've forked out to me if they've lost your ten thousand quid.

CHARLIE You've got a sadistic sense of humour you have...

(RUPERT *and* CYNTHIA *enter from french window holding hands. They don't see* CHARLIE *and* JUGG.)

RUPERT Cynthia?

CYNTHIA Yes?

RUPERT I enjoyed that walk.

CYNTHIA So did I.

RUPERT Cynthia – ?

CYNTHIA Yes?

(CHARLIE, *watching* RUPERT *and* CYNTHIA, *puts his arm round* JUGG, *who reacts.*)

RUPERT I don't always enjoy walking.

CYNTHIA Don't you?

RUPERT No, you see, there's walks – and walks.

CYNTHIA Yes.

(JUGG *reacts even more.*)

RUPERT Yes. Yes, with you I enjoy walking.

(CHARLIE *is now tickling* JUGG'S *neck.* JUGG *slaps his hand.* RUPERT *and* CYNTHIA *jump.*)

CHARLIE Yes! Well, I can see we're in the way. I think I'll ring up my chambers. See how the chambermaids are.

(CHARLIE *exits hall downstage.* CYNTHIA *sits on settee.*)

CYNTHIA Where were we?

RUPERT Walking? I'm not keeping you, am I? From the party?

CYNTHIA No, I'd rather –

RUPERT Yes.

CYNTHIA I'd rather have a rest.

RUPERT Yes. (*Sitting on settee.*) It's nice to have a rest after a walk.

CYNTHIA Yes. (*Suddenly.*) Billy –

RUPERT (*Jumping up.*) Where – ?

CYNTHIA (*Quieter.*) Billy –

RUPERT Oh yes?

CYNTHIA You know, Billy, I'm not quite sure where I am with you.

RUPERT That's all right. Sometimes I'm not quite sure myself.

CYNTHIA (*Smiling.*) What are you talking about?

RUPERT (*Sitting on the settee.*) I don't know. But I do know I find you terribly attractive.

(RUPERT *almost kisses her but stops himself.*)

Cynthia, may I ask you something?

(*She nods.*)

RUPERT Well – if I wasn't who you thought I was, but somebody who you don't think I am, would you like me if I was somebody else.

CYNTHIA Whoever you were I'd like you a lot.

RUPERT Would you, would you really?

(RUPERT *goes to kiss her but stops.*)

Cynthia, I know we haven't known each other long but – I have a proposal to make.

CYNTHIA Yes?

RUPERT I – er – need someone –

CYNTHIA Yes?

RUPERT To do my ironing.

CYNTHIA (*Surprised.*) Your ironing?

RUPERT Yes. Oh – and my cooking, too.

CYNTHIA Why don't you hire a daily help?

RUPERT That's no good. What about the nights. I mean – I get terribly lonely.

CYNTHIA Well. Perhaps you need a dog.

RUPERT Ah! but a dog needs a mistress – and so do I. (*Pause.*) Cynthia, do you like children?

CYNTHIA Very much.

RUPERT Well, what I've always thought is – My children must have a mother.

CYNTHIA That sounds feasible.

RUPERT Don't you want your children to have a mother?

CYNTHIA What are you trying to say?

RUPERT I'm trying to say, I'm me and you're you and that's a big difference. And what with me being me – and you being you – it'll be so handy for the children.

CYNTHIA With such a large family oughtn't we to get married first?

RUPERT I don't see why! (*Both rising.*) Good Lord, yes. Darling, you mean –

CYNTHIA Give me two minutes to think about it. Billy, would you really care for me if it wasn't for the money?

RUPERT I – I – fell in love with you the moment I saw you.

CYNTHIA Oh, Billy. (*She kisses him.*)

RUPERT (*Dazed.*) I say – its better than walking isn't it?

CYNTHIA You stay here, my pet. (*Crossing to hall.*) I think it's a marvellous idea to give you ten thousand pounds, Billy.

(*She runs off into hall upstage. leaving* RUPERT *in a daze.*)

RUPERT So do I – Billy I'm not Billy! I'm not getting ten thousand pounds. (*Moving to hall.*) Cynthia!

(CHARLIE *enters from hall downstage.*)

CHARLIE 'Ow'd it go, son?

RUPERT I – I think she loves me.

CHARLIE Marvellous! That settles Weaver and the agreement's already to be signed.

RUPERT And I'm going to tell Mr Hardcastle the truth.

CHARLIE Marvellous – now all we have to do is keep you out of the way – eh?

RUPERT My mind is made up.

CHARLIE You can't do that. You tell the truth and nobody will get nothing. What about Billy? What about me?

RUPERT It's the only thing for a gentleman to do – and even if I'm not a gentleman – I'm going to do it.

(RUPERT *exists into hall upstage.* CHARLIE *crosses to library door, opens it.* JUGG *is kneeling, his eye glued to the keyhole.*)

CHARLIE Jugg – Jugg! Where's Jugg.

(JUGG *falls in* – CHARLIE *looks down and sees him.*) What are you doing down there!

JUGG (*Rising.*) Getting up.

CHARLIE You saw what he said didn't you!

JUGG Have you got any ideas, Mr B?

CHARLIE Well, look, since the sleeping pills were so successful on Winnie, why don't we give Rupert the same treatment?

JUGG 'Fraid I've run out of sleeping pills. On the other hand, we could utilize these knock-out drops.

CHARLIE Knock-out drops!

JUGG Yes.

CHARLIE Will they work?

JUGG Well they do on greyhounds.

CHARLIE Greyhounds!

JUGG Well, sir, sleeping dogs don't bark.

CHARLIE (*Starting to laugh.*) Sleeping dogs don't bark! Ha, ha. I like that.

(JUGG *and* CHARLIE *laugh.*)

JUGG I thought you would. (*Hand out.*) Drop. (JUGG *and* CHARLIE *continue laughing until* CHARLIE *sees that* JUGG *has his hand held out.* CHARLIE *stops laughing and takes pound note from pocket.*)

CHARLIE Why didn't I think of It?

JUGG And now to make Mr Rupert a member of the Kennel Club. (*Taking money.*)

(JUGG *exits into the hall upstage as* BILLY *comes in from library with directory.*)

BILLY CHARLIE, I've finished this. Can I have another one?

CHARLIE Give me that. come here boy I want to talk to you.

BILLY Brr – Brr – Brr – Brr.

CHARLIE What's up with you, Billy. What's the matter mate? What's wrong?

BILLY Brr – Brr – Brr – Brr. (*Stops.*) There's no answer.

CHARLIE And I fell for it. (CHARLIE *takes directory.*) Come here son. I've got some work for you. Your brother's turning awkard. You'll 'ave to be Billy.

BILLY I am Billy, aren't I?

CHARLIE Course you're Billy.

BILLY You 'ad me worried for a moment.

CHARLIE You 'ave me worried all the time.

(JUGG *enters from hall upstage.*)

JUGG Mr Barnet. Mr Rupert is coming up the 'all.

CHARLIE Has he told Hardcastle the truth yet?

JUGG Not yet. I took the liberty of suggesting that Mr 'Ardcastle *might* be in this room.

CHARLIE (*Grabbing* BILLY.) Quick, the cocktail cabinet.

BILLY When can I come out?

CHARLIE Opening time. (*He pushes* BILLY *into cocktail cabinet.*)

CHARLIE Let's 'ope it's not too late. 'Ave you got the pills?

(JUGG *shows him the pills.*)

JUGG I've got the knock-out drops. I suggest we 'ave the brandy and soda ready and waiting.

CHARLIE Good idea. (*Crosses to cabinet and opens doors.*) Billy – give us the brandy.

(BILLY (Double) *hands out bottle of brandy.*) Now give me the soda.

(*A stream of soda squirts from the cabinet into* CHARLIE'S *face, making his hat wet.*)

The syphon!

(*The syphon is passed out and* CHARLIE *puts the brandy and soda on the table, as* RUPERT *enters from hall upstage.*)

RUPERT Jugg said I'd find Mr Hardcastle in here.

CHARLIE (*Crossing and putting his arm round* RUPERT.) No, son, he was here, but he's gone into the ballroom.

(RUPERT *sees* CHARLIE'S *wet hat.*)

RUPERT Is it raining, Mr Barnet?

CHARLIE No I went into the pool and forgot to take me hat off.

RUPERT Oh, no hard feelings, Mr Barnet!

CHARLIE Of course not. Have a drink to celebrate.

(*There is a delay as* JUGG *gets his finger stuck in the pill tube. Eventually he puts a pill into one of glasses. Meanwhile* CHARLIE *keeps* RUPERT *talking.*)

RUPERT Well, I'm glad you're taking it this way.

CHARLIE (*Aside to* JUGG.) Which one is it.?

JUGG Middle one.

(RUPERT *goes to pick up the wrong glass.*)

CHARLIE No I think this one's a bit cracked. (*Swopping glasses.*) I'll 'ave that. We don't want you coming to no 'arm.

(*He hands drink to* JUGG *then sees that* RUPERT *has picked a drink leaving* CHARLIE *with the doped one.*)

(*Quickly.*) I think you've got mine. No that's yours and this is mine – no –

(CHARLIE *switches glasses round.*)

JUGG Mr Barnet do you mind. (*Switching glasses.*) This is mine, this is yours and this is Mr Rupert's.

CHARLIE (*Getting flustered.*) No, no – keep out of this. (CHARLIE *tries to sort the glasses out, but is now in a hopeless mess.* RUPERT *picks one.*)

RUPERT This one'll do me.

CHARLIE I sincerely hope so.

JUGG Are you going to propose a toast, Mr Barnet.

CHARLIE (*Taking remaining glass.*) For what we are about to receive....

(*They drink –* JUGG *throws drink over his shoulder.* CHARLIE *anxiously studies* RUPERT.)

(*Nervously.*) You feelin' all right?

RUPERT Perfectly.

CHARLIE (*Sinking into armchair.*) I've nobbled meself. I'll get hydrophobia.

RUPERT Well, now I must get down to business.

JUGG (*Panic stricken.*) Are you sure you feel O.K.?

RUPERT Of course. (*He starts to sway.*) Oh!

CHARLIE (*Brightening up.*) That's better. You do look a bit funny.

RUPERT I do feel a fit bunny.

CHARLIE A fit bunny?

(RUPERT *collapses into* JUGG'S *arms.* JUGG *picks him up fireman's fashion.*)

CHARLIE (*Opening cabinet.*) This way to the tomb. (JUGG *deposits* RUPERT *in cabinet. There is a loud and long crash.* JUGG *comes out of cabinet.*) [NOTE. *It is strongly advised that these off-stage crashes are very loud. A small dustbin full of broken bottles and tin cans poured into another dustbin makes an excellent noise!*]

JUGG I knocked over a glass.

(*Laughter comes from the cabinet.*)

CHARLIE Come on, Billy. Out you come, son.

(BILLY *staggers out of cabinet with a gin bottle in his hand.*)

CHARLIE Not you, Rupert.

BILLY No, no. It's me, Charlie.

(BILLY *stands there hiccuping. He is happily intoxicated.*)

CHARLIE (*Horrified.*) Billy! What 'ave you been and gone and done?

BILLY I've been and gone and polished off half a bottle of lemonade.

CHARLIE That's not lemonade – that's gin.

BILLY Gin? Gin – gin! (*He takes a swig.*)

CHARLIE Give me that.

JUGG What are we going to do. One doped 'Ickory Wood in there and one drunk one out 'ere.

(CHARLIE *places gin bottle back in cabinet.* BILLY *crosses up* C. *and has taken a rose from vase.*)

BILLY Jugg – would you care to say a few words to the B.B.C.?

CHARLIE What we gonna do?

JUGG If 'Ardcastle sees him like this he might change 'is mind about the ten thousand.

CHARLIE We'll 'ave to sober 'im up – and quick.

JUGG I know. Black coffee.

BILLY Black coffee!

(JUGG *crosses to refectory table to get coffee.*)

CHARLIE Billy, you're drunk.

BILLY I am not drunk! and to prove it, I'll ring up the A.A.

CHARLIE The A.A.?

(BILLY *picks up the phone on table up* C.)

BILLY Brr – Brr – Brr – 'Ullo. Give me the Alcoholics Anonymous.

(JUGG *crosses back to* BILLY *with coffee and rings a small handbell.*)

JUGG Coffee, for Mr 'Ickory Wood. Chicory for Hickory.

(JUGG *rings the bell again.* BILLY *picks up banana from fruit bowl.*)

BILLY (*Holding banana to other ear.*) Hang on, I'm on the other line. . . . .

CHARLIE Put that down. Drink that up.

(BILLY *takes it and stirs it with banana, and pushes it into protesting* JUGG'S *mouth.* CHARLIE *forces some down him.*)

CHARLIE Billy. 'Ow do you feel!

(BILLY *hiccups.*)

JUGG — I know, get him into the garden and give him some fresh air.

(CHARLIE *and* JUGG *grab* BILLY *who is still drinking coffee and linking their arms through his walk him backwards towards french windows.* BILLY *goes with them but his feet stay behind. They try again.* BILLY *is trying to grab the bottle from table. Finally he gets it.)*

CHARLIE — No! Let's just walk 'im up and down in 'ere. (*They walk* BILLY *up and down stage.* BILLY *has lifted his legs and is getting a free ride.*)

BILLY — (*Singing.*) Daisy, Daisy, give me your answer do . . .

CHARLIE — (*To* BILLY.) This is no good. He's having a free ride – Billy, 'ow d'you feel now?

(BILLY *flings his arms round* CHARLIE'S *neck as his feet give way.*)

BILLY — Lovely.

JUGG — I know – Alka-Seltzer.

BILLY — (*Singing.*) Alka Seltzer. Speedy Alka-Seltzer!

(JUGG *goes to refectory table right. Comes over with tablets. He squirts soda into glass.*)

CHARLIE — (*Taking Alka-Seltzer tablets.*) Billy, swallow that.

JUGG — (*With soda.*) And drink this.

(BILLY *takes a mouthful, but cannot swallow it because he starts to giggle. And then bursts out laughing, spraying soda all over* CHARLIE. JUGG *squirts more soda into glass. Gives* BILLY *the second glass of soda and retreats.* BILLY *drinks soda. He holds the tablet up and surveys it at arms length. He goes cross-eyed looking at it. He closes right eye and attempts to put the tablet into his mouth. In the end he gets it into his eye – monacle fashion.* BILLY *can't understand where the tablet has got to.* CHARLIE *removes it.*)

Charlie — Stick your tongue out.

(BILLY *does so.* CHARLIE *drops tablet, but* BILLY *pulls his tongue in and tablet falls to floor.*)

CHARLIE — Watch me! Billy – like this!

(CHARLIE *puts his tongue out and puts tablet on it.* BILLY *looks at him, giggles and slaps* CHARLIE *on the back.* CHARLIE *chokes and swallows tablet.*)

JUGG — (*Severely.*) Mr 'Ickory Wood! Hold out your tongue.

(BILLY *does so.* CHARLIE *selects another tablet and motions to* JUGG *to stand by with syphon. The stand either side of* BILLY. CHARLIE *stamps on* BILLY'S *foot.* BILLY *opens his mouth, lets out a yell and* CHARLIE *pops the tablet in.* JUGG *squirts soda in and they both smack him on the back. The tablet shoots out.*)

[*N.B. For all this business large peppermints should be used.*]

JUGG — Mr Hickory Wood – 'Ow do you feel now?

(BILLY *burps and giggles.*)

BILLY — Wet.

JUGG — I know – Icecubes down the back of his neck.

(JUGG *crosses to cocktail cabinet.*)

CHARLIE — Ice down the back of his neck. (*Slapping* BILLY'S *face.*) Billy!

(CHARLIE *undoes* BILLY'S *tie and collar.* BILLY *starts to box* CHARLIE. CHARLIE *is attempting to defend himself.* BILLY *fakes with his left hand and brings his right hand down on* CHARLIE'S *hat knocking it well down over his eyes.* JUGG *gets ice bucket from cabinet. He crosses to* BILLY *and slaps it down the back of his neck.* BILLY *jumps, lets out a yell as the icecubes slip down his back.*)

BILLY — Oh-h-h-h!

(BILLY *starts to jump and wriggle in a wild manner.* PIPER *enters from hall upstage.* CHARLIE *joins* BILLY *and copies his wild movements.* JUGG *comes down the other side of* BILLY *and joins in, trying to make it look like a dance.* PIPER *watches in amazement, then joins in.* PIPER *drops the agreement. As he turns to pick it up,* BILLY *squirts the soda syphone at his backside.* PIPER *stops short, feels his trousers.* PIPER *exits hall upstage as* WINNIE *enters* L. *of hall downstage.*)

WINNIE (*Yawning.*) Has anybody seen my Billy? Oh, hello, love I'm that tired. Can't we go up to bed.

BILLY Winnie, luv.

(WINNIE *crosses to armchair. Down* R. *Sits.* BILLY *crosses to* WINNIE *and sits on her lap. Down* R.)

CHARLIE No, you – can't go to bed – we can't 'ave 'em seen in this state.

JUGG We can't have 'em seen in any state.

CHARLIE You'd better go into the library.

BILLY I'd rather go to bed.

CHARLIE And I'd rather you went into the library.

(CHARLIE *and* JUGG *push them into library and close the door.*)

JUGG There's a door leading from the library into the hall – I'll go and lock it.

(JUGG *exits into hall downstage.* BILLY (Double) *and* WINNIE *try to get out of library.*)

WINNIE (*Yawning in doorway.*) Charlie, Charlie, I haven't got a nightie.

CHARLIE You don't need a nightie.

(CHARLIE *pushes them back into the library.* RUPERT *staggers out of the cocktail cabinet.* JUGG *returns from the hall downstage – crosses to cocktail cabinet when he sees* RUPERT *staggering out.*)

RUPERT I say, Mr Barnet.

JUGG This way, Mr Rupert.

RUPERT No I don't want to go –

(JUGG *pushes* RUPERT *back into cabinet and there is a loud crash.*)

JUGG Oh! Me Brandy.

(*The library door is being pushed and* CHARLIE *is desperately trying to hold it.* CLIFTON *enters from hall upstage. Suddenly both the library door and cocktail cabinet are being pushed by* (Doubles) *alternately.* CHARLIE *and* JUGG *holding them both back.*)

[NOTE. *Off-stage the Principal Actor is now changing into his role of* MICHAEL.]

CLIFTON Have you seen Mr Hickory Wood?

CHARLIE Just popping in and out.

CLIFTON Cynthia's just told me of their engagement.

CHARLIE Send him a good luck telegram.

CLIFTON On the contrary, Mr Barnet. I intend to have it out with him tonight.

(CLIFTON *exits hall upstage.*)

CHARLIE Oh, blimey.

(*The library door is pushed.* JUGG *crosses to help* CHARLIE. *The cocktail cabinet opens and* RUPERT (Double) *starts to stagger out.*)

CHARLIE No, you deal with that one. I'll manage 'ere.

BILLY (*Off* (Double).) Charlie! Charlie!

(JUGG *pushes* RUPERT (Double) *back in.* PIPER *enters the hall downstage.* JUGG *has pressed his back against cabinet.* CHARLIE *is trying to look nonchalant while holding the library door.*)

PIPER Oh, Mr Barnet, is Mr Hickory Wood ready to sign the agreement?

CHARLIE Yes.

PIPER Splendid. (PIPER *moves to go. The library door is pushed extra hard.*)

CHARLIE Get back!

PIPER (*Turning.*) I beg your pardon?

CHARLIE I said did you get back.

PIPER Back where from?

CHARLIE From where you've been.

PIPER I haven't been.

CHARLIE You haven't been? Well, you should 'ave.

PIPER Really, Mr Barnet.

(PIPER *exits into hall downstage.* RUPERT (Double) *half pushes himself out of cabinet.* JUGG *closes the door on him, catching feet and arms in door. The library door is being pushed and* BILLY (Double) *appears.*)

CHARLIE You stay in there. Ain't there a key to this perishin' door.

JUGG I've got one somewhere.

(*The scene continues with* BILLY'S *and* RUPERT'S (Double) *arms and legs appearing from cabinet and library and* CHARLIE *and* JUGG *charging back and forth. At the height of the scene the library and cabinet doors are opening and being shut at a furious rate when from the garden comes the sound of laughter. The laughter gets louder and a young man, laughing uproarioulsy enters through the french windows. He is wearing a loud check overcoat and smokes a pipe. It is another identical Hickory Wood. They turn and see the newcomer. Each does a double take.* CHARLIE *and* JUGG *sink to the floor.*)

CURTAIN

ACT THREE

Scene–as before. The action is continuous. CHARLIE *is hurriedly locking the library door.* MICHAEL *is still laughing.*

MICHAEL (*Irish.*) Sure, you're the funniest pair of comedians I've ever come across.

CHARLIE I'm seeing things!

MICHAEL I haven't laughed so much since the O'Malley boys married the Shaunnesy twins. Ah–there was a devil of a mix-up. Those two boys got so drunk on their wedding night, they couldn't tell those two lovely girls apart. (*He laughs.*)

JUGG 'Ighly comical.

MICHAEL In fact they're not sure to this day if it did work out right.

CHARLIE (*Gaping.*) I don't believe it!

MICHAEL Sure 'tis true. And if there was an error those two girls have never let on. Bless their darlin' hearts.

JUGG Never mind about them. What about your kisser.

MICHAEL Why it's the face I was born with.

CHARLIE I'm not going to like the answer but–who are you?

MICHAEL Michael Hickory Wood from Ireland.

JUGG Was your father a commercial traveller?

MICHAEL Sure I never saw the old gentleman. He went on the rocks before I was born and I was brought up by my dear old Uncle Patrick. Ah me dear old Uncle Patrick. A darlin' man. You'll see it on his tombstone to this day. Never lied, never cheated, never smoked, tee-total all his life and finally passed peacefully away dead drunk smokin' marijuana in a jail in Hong Kong.

JUGG That's how we'll finish up.

CHARLIE Jugg, post yourself outside in the hall and don't let nobody in.

(JUGG *holds out his hand.*)

JUGG Under the circumstances sentry duty will be a costly item.

(CHARLIE *forks out.*)

JUGG You know, I wouldn't have bothered with the dog's if I'd known I was going to make a fortune on the treble chance. (JUGG *exits hall.*)

MICHAEL Sure, that was a devil of a lot of money you gave that Leprchaun.

(*He gives* CHARLIE *back the money.*)

CHARLIE How did you get that.

MICHAEL Part-time conjuror, entertainer and pickpocket–your wallet!

(*He hands* CHARLIE *his wallet.*)

CHARLIE Anything else?

MICHAEL Let me see–(*He feels in his pockets.*)–Your socks! (*He hands them to* CHARLIE *who pulls up his trousers–and reveals his bare ankles.*) And now, me boyo, to business.

CHARLIE There ain't gonna be no business.

MICHAEL Sh-h-h-h the wee folk.

CHARLIE Eh? The what?

MICHAEL The wee folk–they might be listening.

(MICHAEL *tiptoes to archway and quietly lifts curtain, revealing* JUGG'S *feet.* MICHAEL *takes warming pan off wall (down* R.*) and hits* JUGG *through curtain.* JUGG *enters hall upstage in a completely dazed condition.*)

JUGG You rang, Madam?

(JUGG *staggers out upstage of hall.*)

MICHAEL (*To* CHARLIE.) And now to the purpose of me visit. I read this notice in the *Dublin Echo* and left straightways to see what's in it for me.

CHARLIE Nothink!

MICHAEL Well, if that isn't kind of you but I've been listening outside the window for the past 'alf hour.

CHARLIE You've been listening outside the window . . .

MICHAEL And my presence here would be most embarrassing for the lot of you. Especially if I was to let out that there's *three* of us!

CHARLIE Not so loud.

MICHAEL (*Shouting*.) Triplets!

CHARLIE Shhh! All right, if you'll scarper I'll give you–ten per cent.

MICHAEL It's a tempting offer. I'm overwhelmed. You've touched me here–but I'd rather have the lot.

CHARLIE Eh?

MICHAEL I intend to pass myself off as my brother Billy. Have the ten thousand and the girl to boot.

CHARLIE Oh!

(CLIFTON *enters from hall upstage.*)

CLIFTON Ah, Mr Hickory Wood!

CHARLIE (*To* MICHAEL.) Billy, this is one of Miss Cynthia's guests. He wants to see you. He's an *art* specialist.

MICHAEL (*With hand over heart.*) I'm feeling perfectly well, thank you, Doctor.

(CHARLIE *laughs falsely.*)

CLIFTON (*Shaking* MICHAEL's *hand.*) So we meet at last.

MICHAEL Dr Livingstone, I presume?

CLIFTON No, Clifton Weaver. I suppose I should offer you my congratulations.

MICHAEL Congratulations?

CLIFTON On your success with Cynthia.

MICHAEL Cynthia! It's the blarney, you know.

CLIFTON Well, I trust the best man won.

MICHAEL I'm sure he did.

CLIFTON However, to business.

MICHAEL Business?

CLIFTON Your painting.

MICHAEL My painting? Which one would that be now?

CLIFTON We'll talk about it now, Mr Barnet. (*To* MICHAEL.) I'm referring to your portrait of Miss Amy.

MICHAEL Ah! Me portrait of Miss Amy

CLIFTON Yes. There seemed to be a certain confliction of styles. What influence would you say you were under?

MICHAEL Drink, most of the time.

CLIFTON (*Smiling.*) Yes–an occupational hazard. Well, let's lay our cards on the table, shall we?

MICHAEL A pack of cards! We'll use mine.

(MICHAEL *produces a pack of cards and manipulates them expertly up his arm.*)

CLIFTON No, no. To business. Having studied the portrait most carefully I come to only one conclusion–

CHARLIE Yes, but–

CLIFTON –Mr Hickory Wood has great talent.

CHARLIE Yes, Mr Hickory Wood has great–talent?

CLIFTON And I'd like to commission a painting from him for my Art Gallery. Shall we say one hundred pounds?

MICHAEL One hundred pounds. Lovely!

CHARLIE But this isn't–

MICHAEL Isn't what, me boyo?

CHARLIE Isn't my lucky day, is it?

CLIFTON I have a cheque here for one hundred pounds.

CHARLIE Eh?

CLIFTON If you wouldn't mind signing this receipt.

MICHAEL Not at all, at all. Your pen, Charlie, and your back.

(*He takes pen from* CHARLIE'S *top pocket, takes receipt and signs it on* CHARLIE'S *back. Dotting his full stop which makes* CHARLIE *jump.*)

MICHAEL A pleasure to do business with you, Mr Weaver.

(MICHAEL *pats him on shoulder as* WEAVER *puts receipt in wallet.*)

CLIFTON And with you. I shall see you anon.

(WEAVER *exits hall upstage.*)

MICHAEL Ah! The luck of the Irish.

CHARLIE One hundred pounds–For that painting. What do I get out of it?

MICHAEL By way of commission–Mr Weaver's wallet.

(MICHAEL *gives* CHARLIE *wallet.*)

CHARLIE Give me that! I'm in enough trouble already.

(CHARLIE *is holding wallet as* CLIFTON *re-enters upstage.*)

CLIFTON Do you mind, Mr Barnet.

(CLIFTON *takes wallet and exits upstage.*)

MICHAEL And now for the impersonation of me brother Billy.

CHARLIE You can't impersonate Billy.

MICHAEL Why not?

CHARLIE Your Irish accent for one thing.

MICHAEL Ah, to be sure, me Irish accent. (*Imitating* BILLY.) I wouldn't worry about that, Charlie.

CHARLIE Here–what about your togs? My two Billys are dressed up to the 'nines'.

MICHAEL Togs. 'Tis but a minor detail. (*Eyeing* CHARLIE'S *dress-suit.*) You know, I think it would be better if we were to continue our little conversation outside–er–just in case one of the family should come along.

(MICHAEL *looks out of hallway.*)

CHARLIE (*A gleam in his eye.*) A good idea. We'll be alone out there.

(*Unseen by* MICHAEL, CHARLIE *picks up a long-handled fire shovel and holds it behind his back.*)

MICHAEL I'm sure we'll come to an amicable solution. (*Unseen by* CHARLIE, MICHAEL *picks up a brass poker and holds it behind his back.*) And don't worry, me boyo, I knows where I can lay me hands on a darlin' dress-suit. (*They both laugh and go out into garden.* HARDCASTLE *and a protesting* JUGG *enter hall upstage.*)

JUGG For twenty years I've taken care of you and I say–(*Looking around nervously.*)–this room is too cold for you.

HARDCASTLE It's as warm as toast.

JUGG That's what I mean, sir–too 'ot.

HARDCASTLE My brandy's beginning to affect you, Jugg. You'll be hearing things next.

(*From the garden comes a thud and a groan.* HARDCASTLE *and* JUGG *look at each other.*)

HARDCASTLE What was that?

JUGG I don't know, sir. I'll go and investigate.

HARDCASTLE (*To himself.*) I've got a feeling there's summat going on 'ere what I don't know about. (JUGG *re-enters from garden with bent poker.*)

JUGG Couldn't see no one, sir–only this.

HARDCASTLE That didn't grow in my garden.

JUGG No, we don't grow red-hot pokers do we!

HARDCASTLE Where's Hickory Wood!

JUGG He might be in two or three places.

HARDCASTLE Well, go and find him then.

JUGG Very good, sir.

(HARDCASTLE *takes out agreement and reads it.* CHARLIE *enters french windows in underpants and in dumb show asks* JUGG *for clothes.* CHARLIE *hides behind screen.* JUGG *exits into hall downstage as* CYNTHIA *and* PIPER *enter hall upstage talking.*)

CYNTHIA Ah! There you are, Poddy!

PIPER I see you have the agreement, Mr Hardcastle.

HARDCASTLE Nowt to do now but get Billy to sign it.

(RUPERT *staggers from cocktail cabinet.*)

RUPERT Oh, Oh, my head!

HARDCASTLE By gum, you're a keen drinker.

RUPERT No–no . . .

CYNTHIA (*Taking* RUPERT's *arm.*) Daddy's delighted with our news, darling.

RUPERT What news is that?

CYNTHIA That we're engaged. Remember?

RUPERT Oh, yes–I seem to have been out of touch with things.

HARDCASTLE All this nonsense. Come and get this agreement signed.

PIPER One moment, sir. Now all I need is a witness, Miss Cynthia if you'll sit here.

RUPERT There's something I must tell you. I am not . . .

PIPER One moment.

HARDCASTLE Now what?

PIPER As you'll see here–

(CYNTHIA, RUPERT *and* HARDCASTLE *settle round table.* PIPER *is pointing out items in the agreement.* JUGG *enters hall downstage with clothes, and gives them to* CHARLIE *behind screen and crosses to the settee.* HARDCASTLE *sees him.* JUGG *pretends to dust the settee.*)

JUGG I was polishing the pouffe.

(JUGG *exits hallway downstage.*)

PIPER As I was about to say, although we all know that Mr Hickory Wood is, in actual fact, Mr Hickory Wood, proof of his identity would save a lot of trouble.

HARDCASTLE What d'you want then?

PIPER If we could have his birth certificate that would supply the necessary proof.

HARDCASTLE (*To* RUPERT.) Have you got your birth certificate?

RUPERT Mr Hardcastle, you're labouring under a misapprehension.

(CHARLIE'S *head appears above screen, and threatens* RUPERT *with fire shovel. Seeing he's too far away to hit* RUPERT, CHARLIE *disappears behind screen.*)

RUPERT You see I am not.

HARDCASTLE Not what?

RUPERT Well, you see–I have a birth certificate, but it won't be necessary because I'm not . . .

(CHARLIE *moves screen down to where* RUPERT *has been standing, but* RUPERT *has moved* L. to PIPER. CHARLIE *goes to hit* RUPERT, *but seeing he's moved, disappears behind screen again.*)

PIPER On the contrary, Mr Hickory Wood, I feel it's most necessary.

(RUPERT *moves back to* HARDCASTLE.)

RUPERT Mr Hardcastle, I must confess, you see, I'm not . . .

(CHARLIE *has moved screen over to* L. *Unfortunately he is not aware that* RUPERT *has moved back again and the shovel crashes down on* PIPER. CHARLIE *crosses back upstage with screen,* PIPER *staggers on to the settee.*)

HARDCASTLE What's the matter with you?

PIPER (*Shaking head and looking up.*) Something struck me.

HARDCASTLE Well, let's hear it then.

PIPER No, no–something struck me.

CYNTHIA Are you all right, Mr Piper.

PIPER Yes, thank you–yes.

HARDCASTLE All this larking about. Come and get this thing signed.

(CHARLIE *appears from behind screen. He is now dressed in hunting outfit. Hunting coat, cap and riding jodphurs. He still carries the fire shovel.*)

RUPERT Mr Hardcastle I really must–

CHARLIE (*From behind screen with forced cheerfulness.*) 'ullo, 'ullo, 'ullo.

HARDCASTLE Barnet, what are you doing dressed up like that for?

CHARLIE I've just been to a stag party.

RUPERT Mr Hardcastle–I really–must–

CYNTHIA (*To* RUPERT.) Have you got your birth certificate, darling?

(CHARLIE *threatens* RUPERT *with shovel.* CHARLIE *takes off coat, hat and throws them behind screen. He is now dressed in Jodphurs and sports shirt.*)

RUPERT (*Glancing anxiously at* CHARLIE.) Yes–er–I think it's upstairs.

HARDCASTLE Well, go and get it then.

RUPERT Cynthia–

CYNTHIA Yes, darling?

RUPERT (*Perplexed.*) Don't let anyone who looks like me sign that, will you?

CYNTHIA No, darling.

HARDCASTLE And hurry up!

RUPERT Yes, darling.

(RUPERT *exits hall downstage. There is a furious knocking from library door.*)

BILLY (Double) (*Off library.*) Charlie! Charlie!

(CHARLIE *laughs and looks around.*)

HARDCASTLE What's that noise–?

CYNTHIA It's Billy, isn't it?

HARDCASTLE I thought he went upstairs. Get him out.

BILLY (*Off.*) Stand back!

(CHARLIE *unlocks library door as* BILLY *propels himself against it and falls right into* HARDCASTLE'S *lap.*)

CHARLIE Highly entertaining, Billy.

CYNTHIA Darling, I thought you were going upstairs.

BILLY What for?

HARDCASTLE To get your birth certificate?

BILLY Why? I've got it on me.

PIPER Thank you. (*He takes certificate.*)

BILLY Aye, I've got a birthmark as well–I can always tell who I am just by looking at that.

HARDCASTLE Where it it?

BILLY What?

HARDCASTLE Your birthmark.

BILLY I'm sitting on it.

(HARDCASTLE *pushes* BILLY *off his lap.* WINNIE *enters the library.*)

WINNIE Ah . . .

CHARLIE Oh, blimey, she's woken up.

WINNIE I'll slaughter you, Charlie Barnet. Locked me up in the library, he did.

HARDCASTLE Locked you up, Mrs. Barnet!

WINNIE I'm not Mrs Barnet.

HARDCASTLE (*Placating her.*) No, of course, you're not. Why don't you go and lie down.

WINNIE I'm not leaving my Billy. (*To* BILLY.) Go on, you tell them.

BILLY Aye, but Winnie, luv.

CHARLIE (*To* WINNIE *aloud.*) Go and lie down, my dear. (*He smiles round room.*)

WINNIE Go on, Billy, what we decided.

BILLY Well . . . you see, Winnie says I've got to tell the truth about . . .

(*A hand* (MICHAEL'S Double) *appears* (*holding pipe*) *round the library door and the lights suddenly go out. In the blackout Principal Actor takes pipe from* Double, *and assumes part of* MICHAEL. BILLY (Double) *is pushed into cocktail cabinet and there is a loud crash.*)

CHARLIE Somebody's having a drink.

PIPER What's happened to the lights?

HARDCASTLE They've gone out.

PIPER It's all right I've found the switch, Mr Hardcastle.

(CYNTHIA *switches the light on again.* PIPER *has hold of* HARDCASTLE'S *ear.*)

HARDCASTLE Get your finger out of my earhole.

(*Everything is as before except* MICHAEL, *smoking pipe, has replaced* BILLY.)

HARDCASTLE I don't know what's going on here tonight.

CYNTHIA (*Coldly.*) Billy was just about to tell us the truth about something.

WINNIE (*Triumphantly.*) Aye.

MICHAEL (*In Yorkshire.*) Tell me the truth? Aye, the truth is I'm delighted that Mr Hardcastle 'as done me the honour of allowing 'is lovely daughter to become my betrothed.

CYNTHIA (*Sitting.*) Oh, darling.

WINNIE (*Wailing.*) Oh-h-h-h!

(WINNIE *runs out into hall downstage.*)

HARDCASTLE By gum, Barnet, you've got a lot to put up with there. Come on, Piper, get the money out.

MICHAEL (*Yorkshire.*) I'll look after Cynthia, Mr 'Ardcastle and see she never wants for nowt.

CHARLIE (*Arm round* MICHAEL.) That's my boy.

MICHAEL (*In Irish aside to* CHARLIE.) And with ten thousand pounds I'll not be wanting for nowt, either.

CHARLIE Eh?

MICHAEL (*Irish aside to* CHARLIE.) And t'anks for your dress-suit. It's a darlin' fit.

CHARLIE Michael! Where's Billy?

MICHAEL (*Nodding towards cocktail cabinet.*) Sleepin' peacefuly in the cocktail cabinet.

CHARLIE Oh, Gawd!

HARDCASTLE We're ready now. Sign here, Billy.

(PIPER *takes out money.*)

MICHAEL (*Yorkshire.*) I'm going to sign, Charlie.

(MICHAEL *takes pen and goes to sign.* CHARLIE *grabs the agreement.*)

CHARLIE (*Taking pen.*) No! Wait I object, your 'onour . . .

HARDCASTLE What?

CHARLIE I mean, Mr 'Ardcastle–I definitely object.

PIPER Why? (*Putting back money.*)

CHARLIE Why? It's another of them takeover bids.

PIPER 'Take-over' bids?

CHARLIE Yes–you remember the case of–er–Marks versus Spencer?

PIPER Mark's versus Spencer? I can't say I do.

CHARLIE No–no. it was Freeman against 'Ardy and Willis.

PIPER I don't recall that either.

CHARLIE What? Most exciting–Freeman knocked out Willis in the first round–er–Willis was referee. (CHARLIE *boxes* PIPER.)

PIPER (*Defending himself.*) Really, Mr Barnet.

HARDCASTLE If we don't get this signed I'm going to start on the brandy.

(JUGG *enters from hall downstage.* MICHAEL *goes to sign.* PIPER *takes out money.)*

CHARLIE No! (*In mock pain.*) Oh, ah! Ouch!

PIPER What is it now?

(CHARLIE *takes agreement as he passes.*)

CHARLIE (*Hobbling about.*) Me old war wounds playing me up again–ouch! Got bit by a doodle-bug in me left leg.

CYNTHIA Let's sign, Billy, then we can join the dancing.

MICHAEL (*Yorkshire.*) I'd like that. (*Taking agreement.*) Now where do I sign?

JUGG Ladies and Gentlemen–Take your partners for the 'Spot Waltz' competition.

HARDCASTLE Eh?

JUGG The 'Spot Waltz' competition. The first prize is a mink coat.

CYNTHIA How gorgeous. Come on darling.

MICHAEL (*Irish.*) Never mind the ruddy dancing–er– (*Yorkshire.*) What about the agreement?

CYNTHIA It can wait five minutes. This'll be fun–a mink coat.

MICHAEL (*Yorkshire.*) I don't know.

CYNTHIA Please, darling–I've only got a skunk–mink suits me.

CHARLIE (*Aside to* MICHAEL.) And skunk suits you.

PIPER Miss Cynthia, don't you think . . .

CYNTHIA We'll only be a minute. (*To* MICHAEL.) Come on, darling.

MICHAEL (*Lapsing into Irish.*) I know. But the agreement–

(CYNTHIA drags MICHAEL *off* R. *of hall upstage.*)

HARDCASTLE (*Despondently.*) Come on, Piper, let's have a look at this 'Spot Waltz'.

PIPER I really think . . .

HARDCASTLE Shut-up! Find Amy and have a go–you'll look lovely in mink.

(*They exit hall upstage.*)

CHARLIE Jugg, Jugg, that 'Spot Waltz' competition was a masterpiece.

JUGG Thank you, I could see you was playing for time.

CHARLIE It was the mink coat what done it. (*Laughing.*) 'Oo's supplying it–'Ardcastle?

JUGG No, you.

(JUGG *exits library.* CLIFTON *enters french windows and crosses to* CHARLIE.)

CLIFTON Ah, Mr Barnet. I was hoping to find Cynthia here.

CHARLIE Bad luck, son. She's been booked for my Billy.

CLIFTON Really? I think I must disagree. Not after she's seen this little document.

CHARLIE What little document?

CLIFTON (*Taking out document.*) My agreement with Mr Hickory Wood–

CHARLIE Eh?

CLIFTON As his solicitor you'll find it quite valid. I wouldn't wish to perpetrate anything underhand. (WEAVER *shows* CHARLIE *the document.*)

CHARLIE But that's your receipt for one hundred quids worth of painting.

CLIFTON Really, Mr Barnet! A hundred for that rubbish? No, unfortunately, what Mr Hickory Wood actually signed was this agreement with me. (*He holds agreement for* CHARLIE *to read.*)

CHARLIE (*Reading.*) 'I, Billy Hickory Wood, hereby promise to terminate my relationship with Miss Cynthia Hardcastle. In return for which I accept from Mr Clifton Weaver the sum of one hundred pounds.'

(CHARLIE *goes to snatch the agreement, but* WEAVER *puts it back in his wallet.*)

CLIFTON I don't believe Cynthia will feel quite the same about him when she realizes he values her friendship at a paltry one hundred.

CHARLIE But that's not true!

CLIFTON (*Rising.*) This certainly gives the impression that it is, Mr Barnet. All's fair in love and war. When I don't get my way I turn nasty.

CHARLIE I think you went off ages ago.

CLIFTON I didn't come here to be insulted.

JUGG (*Entering from library.*) Where do you usually go, sir?

(WEAVER *turns to* JUGG *as* CHARLIE *snatches wallet from his hand.* WEAVER *advances on* CHARLIE. CHARLIE *throws wallet to* JUGG *who throws it back to* CHARLIE. *This continues until* JUGG *throws the wallet under the bureau.* WEAVER *bends down to pick it up.* CHARLIE *and* JUGG *stamp together. The drawer shoots out as* WEAVER *rises.* WEAVER *bangs his head and sinks to the ground.* CHARLIE *and* JUGG *shake hands.*)

JUGG What a lovely beautiful bang on the Bonce.

(CHARLIE *extracts the agreement from wallet and puts wallet back in* WEAVER'S *pocket.*)

CHARLIE (*To* JUGG.) Well, I've got what I wanted. Is this your department?

JUGG Removal of garbage? I suppose so.

CHARLIE I'll give you a hand. I've put the wallet back in his pocket.

(*They drag* WEAVER *towards library.*)

JUGG I've got him all right. Mr B, do I remind you of that advertisement for cod liver oil? Mr Barnet, do you have the feeling that all this has happened before?

CHARLIE No.

JUGG No. (*Holding hand out.*)

CHARLIE Yes. (CHARLIE *grimaces and forks out wallet.* CHARLIE *opens the library door.*) Seems a lot for a dustman.

JUGG Dustman! Please, Mr Barnet–Refuse Disposal Officer.

(JUGG *drags* WEAVER *off into the library.*)

CHARLIE (*Calling off to* JUGG.) Get rid of him permanently.

(RUPERT *appears downstage of hall.*)

RUPERT I say, Mr Barnet, I don't seem to know what's going on round here.

CHARLIE You're not the only one, son.

RUPERT I've only had one drink all night and I've got the most dreadful hangover and I thought Cynthia was engaged to me, but she's in the ballroom with Billy.

CHARLIE I suppose I may as well put you in the picture. That's not Billy out there–that's Michael.

RUPERT Oh, I see–who's Michael?

CHARLIE Your other twin brother.

RUPERT Mr Barnet, that's too, too much.

CHARLIE It's three too much. (MICHAEL (Double) *sings off* R. *in ballroom 'The Garden Where the Praties Grow'.*)

RUPERT (*At hallway.*) Good Lord. Well, if that's Michael, where's Billy?

CHARLIE (*Pointing to cabinet.*) In the cocktail cabinet.

(JUGG *enters from library singing and wheeling a double-bass case.*)

CHARLIE Blimey, you giving us a concert?

JUGG No, Mr Weaver's leaving early. Go, man go, go, man go–

(JUGG *taps the double–bass case, winks, and exits french windows.*)

CHARLIE (*To* RUPERT.) Let that be a lesson to you, son. Any more nonsense from you and you'll end up in a Glockenspeil to Glynebourne.

(CYNTHIA *enters hall upstage and without seeing* RUPERT *goes over to* CHARLIE.)

CYNTHIA Mr Barnet, Billy's gone too far. He's drinking and flirting with every pretty girl at the dance and singing bawdy Irish songs.

RUPERT (*To her.*) I say–Cynthia.

CYNTHIA How dare you follow me.

RUPERT No, you don't understand.

CYNTHIA Well?

RUPERT I've been trying to explain all evening, darling. I'm not who I said I was–

CYNTHIA Aren't you?

RUPERT No. When I first arrived I said I was who I was. When I met you I had to say I was who I wasn't. Then I had to be who I said I was when I wasn't when I really wanted to be who I was when I said I was. Now I want you to know that I'm not who I said I was when I wasn't but who I was when I said I was who I was.

(*There is a pause.*)

CHARLIE Say that again.

RUPERT When I first arrived–

CHARLIE No!

(MICHAEL (DOUBLE) *is heard singing off–'Dear Old Donegal'.*) There's only one thing for it. Miss Cynthia, come here.

(CHARLIE *leads* CYNTHIA *up to archway and points off towards the ballroom.*)

CYNTHIA Mr Barnet, I've had quite enough–

(CYNTHIA *looks off and double-takes between the ballroom and* RUPERT. *The singing stops.*)

CHARLIE Now look–that's not, 'him, is it?

CYNTHIA I can't believe it, Billy.

RUPERT Ah, now that's the point, I'm not Billy.

CYNTHIA Not Billy?

RUPERT No, Mr Barnet asked me to be, and I didn't know whether to be or not to be.

CHARLIE Quoting Shakespeare won't help.

CYNTHIA Well, if you're not Billy, who on earth are you?

RUPERT I'm–er–(*To* CHARLIE.) Who am I?

CHARLIE I've forgotten myself now–two and two?

CYNTHIA Four.

CHARLIE You're Rupert.

CYNTHIA Rupert!

CHARLIE Billy's twin brother.

RUPERT And that's Michael.

CYNTHIA I'm going to remain quite calm–now you're brother's name is either Billy or Michael.

RUPERT Yes.

CYNTHIA Good.

RUPERT It's both.

CHARLIE Wait a minute–wait a minute. There's three of them.

CYNTHIA (*Sitting on the settee.*) Three of them.

RUPERT So Mr Barnet says–he's the one that's counting.

CYNTHIA But surely you know how many brothers you've got.

RUPERT No I don't. You can't see our family tree for the Hickory Woods.

(*Pause.*)

CYNTHIA (*Rising.*) And I suppose all three of you have been making love to me?

RUPERT (*Kissing her.*) Only me, darling.

CYNTHIA Oh, yes–and which one of you proposed to me?

RUPERT (*Kissing her.*) Only me, darling.

CYNTHIA Oh yes–and I suppose all three of you are after Daddy's money.

CHARLIE (*Kissing her.*) Only me, darling.

RUPERT No, only me, Darling.

(RUPERT *kisses her as* WINNIE *enters hall upstage.*)

WINNIE Oh, he's at it again.

CHARLIE (*Interrupting.*) Silence! Now listen, Winifred, I'll explain it once and no more! (*To* RUPERT.) You made a mess of it the last time. This 'ere is *Rupert*, Billy's brother. I came down 'ere with Billy, Rupert's brother. Rupert takes a 'shine' to Cynthia, who thinks Rupert's Billy. You think Billy's Rupert. Michael turns up and pretends to be Billy. Michael sticks Billy in the cocktail cabinet. Rupert gets asked for Billy's birth certificate. Michael's doing an Irish jig out there. And I'm Charlie!

(*Pause.*)

WINNIE Well, why didn't you say so in the first place?

CHARLIE (*Amazed that she's got it.*) Eh?

WINNIE You mean there's three of them. Rupert loves Cynthia, my Billy loves me–Michael's mucking it all up and you're a proper Charlie.

CHARLIE That's about it. Ten thousand quid up the spout.

CYNTHIA Oh, why?

CHARLIE Because your old man said if there was more than one of them nobody would get nothing.

CYNTHIA But Daddy doesn't know.

CHARLIE But *you* do.

CYNTHIA I don't see why I should tell him.

RUPERT I say, Cynthia, you can't do that.

CYNTHIA All we have to do is get rid of–er–Michael. (*To* RUPERT.) Keep you out of the way, my pet and let Billy sign the agreement.

RUPERT You're marvellous, darling.

CHARLIE Why didn't we let 'er in on it before?

RUPERT Right. The first objective is operation Michael. We must plan this strategically–a military campaign.

CHARLIE And what are your qualifications?

RUPERT I'll have you know I was a sea-rover.

CHARLIE Blimey, this is war–not Bob-a-Job Week.

RUPERT Michael must be speedily eliminated. I'll get hold of Jugg to send him in here.

CHARLIE That'll cost me something.

RUPERT (*To* CYNTHIA.) We can use this rug. As soon as Michael appears you attract his attention while Mr Barnet heaves the rug from under his feet. Understood?

CYNTHIA Yes, my sweet. (*She kisses him.*)

CHARLIE Yes, my sweet. (*He kisses* WINNIE. *She slaps his face.*)

RUPERT Rightio. Synchronize your watches. Zero hour approaching and Dib, Dib, Dib. (*Holding his fingers up in scouts' sign exits hall upstage.*)

CHARLIE You know he'd have been drummed out of the brownies.

CYNTHIA I think it's a very good plan.

WINNIE Aye–better than your sleeping-pills. Oh, here, supposing that Michael goes into the library.

CYNTHIA Oh, yes, then you and Billy must repeat the process in there.

WINNIE Good idea. Eh, where is my Billy?

CHARLIE Oh, blimey, I'd forgotton 'im. 'E's still in the cocktail cabinet–it's become a sort of Hickory Wood family seat. Come on Billy, out you come son.

(*He opens cocktail cabinet and* BILLY *staggers out.*)

BILLY Mr Hardcastle, Winnie says I've got to tell the truth–

CHARLIE Wake up.

BILLY I am awake–I'm very sorry, Cynthia–

CHARLIE Wrap up. Take 'im in there, Winnie and explain about Michael.

BILLY Who's Michael?

CHARLIE Your twin brother.

BILLY I thought that were Rupert.

CHARLIE Don't start again–I can't bear it.

BILLY I don't like being in the dark.

CHARLIE You've been there for years.

BILLY I like to know what's what.

CHARLIE Well look it up in 'Who's Who'.

(CHARLIE *pushes* BILLY *and* WINNIE *into the library.*)

CYNTHIA Oh, Mr Barnet, isn't Billy sweet.

CHARLIE Love–be 'appy with the brother you've got.

CYNTHIA Don't worry, Mr Barnet, I am.

CHARLIE Right, let's 'ave a rehearsal.

(CYNTHIA *pulls carpet and* CHARLIE *falls to the floor.*)

CHARLIE No, I pull the rug while you attract his attention. Look out, Michael, action stations!!

(CYNTHIA *sits on settee*–CHARLIE *stands by carpet.* RUPERT *enters from hall upstage.*)

RUPERT I can't seem to find Jugg anywhere . . .

(CHARLIE *pulls the mat,* RUPERT *falls to the ground.* CHARLIE *and* CYNTHIA *shakes hands.*)

CYNTHIA Well done Mr Barnet. It's Rupert!

CHARLIE (*Horrified.*) You sure?

(CYNTHIA *bends over and kisses* RUPERT.)

CYNTHIA Positive.

(CHARLIE *goes to kiss* RUPERT.)

CHARLIE I'll take your word for it. (*Slaps* RUPERT'S *face.*)

HARDCASTLE (*Off.*) Come on, Billy lad, step on the gas, Jugg.

CHARLIE Your old man with Michael!

CYNTHIA Quick the cocktail cabinet.

CHARLIE 'Ome from 'ome.

RUPERT (*In a daze.*) I've spent half the night in there.

(*They push* RUPERT *into cocktail cabinet and there is a loud crash.*)

[NOTE. *Principal Actor now prepares to enter from hall as* MICHAEL *smoking pipe.*]

CHARLIE Don't bother to wash up.

CYNTHIA What are we going to do?

CHARLIE Stall.

CYNTHIA What about Billy and Winnie?

CHARLIE Oh, blimey. (*He dashes to library door.*) Hang on in there, you two. There's been a counter attack.

(JUGG *pushes* HARDCASTLE *on from hall upstage.* PIPER *and* MICHAEL *follow.*)

HARDCASTLE Well, didn't think much of 'Spot Waltz' competition.

MICHAEL (*Yorkshire.*) This is a very proud moment for me, Mr Hardcastle. A proud moment. (*To* CHARLIE *in Irish.*) Hello there, me boyo.

HARDCASTLE You know, love. He's right gone on you, lass. You should hear the things he's been saying about you.

CHARLIE And you should hear the thing we've been saying about him.

(JUGG *places carpet runner back up* C.)

PIPER Do you think we can settle this now, Mr Hardcastle?

(*They settle round the table.*)

CHARLIE (*Aside to* JUGG.) Jugg, quick, the knock-out drops for Michael.

JUGG One Mickey O'Finn coming up.

(JUGG *holds out his hand and* CHARLIE *forks out.*)

CHARLIE I'll be glad when the racing season's over.

(JUGG *exits hall downstage.*)

HARDCASTLE Barnet, come and see that Billy signs in the right place.

CYNTHIA No, let's wait until Jugg gets back.

HARDCASTLE Jugg? 'E's only the butler.

CHARLIE 'E might be the butler to you but he's a godsend to me.

(CHARLIE *surreptitiously takes the agreement.*)

HARDCASTLE Let's get the agreement signed. Where is it?

CHARLIE Don't say you've lost the agreement!

(PIPER *takes out money.* CHARLIE *shows agreement to* MICHAEL *and then deftly stuffs it in his trousers.*)

HARDCASTLE Where's the flaming agreement?

PIPER There's a draft in the library.

CHARLIE I'll shut the door.

PIPER A draft copy of the agreement.

MICHAEL (*Rising.*) I'll get it. (MICHAEL *exits into the library.*)

CHARLIE I'll come with you. (*Aside to* CYNTHIA.) We can't wait for Jugg.

(CHARLIE *dashes into library, taking the warming-pan as he goes.*)

HARDCASTLE (*To* CYNTHIA.) You know, love, he's right struck on you.

(*There is a loud gong from the library.*)

HARDCASTLE What was that?

(CYNTHIA *quickly crosses to library door.*)

CYNTHIA Ten-thirty.

PIPER I make it only ten-twenty.

CYNTHIA You'll have to get that library clock seen to, Daddy.

HARDCASTLE We haven't got a clock in the library.

CYNTHIA It's time we had one then.

(BILLY *and* CHARLIE *come in from the library.*)

CHARLIE (*To* BILLY.) Winnie'll look after Michael.

BILLY Aye, but you didn't introduce me.

HARDCASTLE Who to?

BILLY My other brother.

CHARLIE (*Quickly.*) My grandmother.

HARDCASTLE Your grandmother–what's she doing in t'library.

BILLY Reading to grandfather.

HARDCASTLE Grandfather?

CHARLIE Yus, they've gone 'ome now.

HARDCASTLE By gum, I never get to meet half the people in this house.

CHARLIE Thank Gawd for that! 'Ere's the agreement.

PIPER (*Taking agreement.*) Splendid. Now all I need is a witness. Miss Hardcastle, will you stand on my right. Mr Hickory Wood on my left. I shall stand in the middle.

HARDCASTLE You're not performing the wedding ceremony. (*To* CYNTHIA.) Are you ready, lass?

CYNTHIA Yes, daddy.

HARDCASTLE Ready, lad?

BILLY Yes, daddy.

(HARDCASTLE *reacts.* JUGG *enters hall downstage with glass of brandy, into which he tips a pill and comes to* HARDCASTLE'S *left.*)

PIPER If you'll sign there, Miss Hardcastle.

JUGG (*To* BILLY.) Would you care for a small brandy first, sir?

BILLY Eh–oh aye.

JUGG It's Napoleon.

CHARLIE (*Rising–suddenly realizing.*) Not tonight, Josephine!

JUGG (*Aside to* CHARLIE.) That's full of dog dope.

CHARLIE (*Aside to* JUGG.) You've nobbled the favourite.

JUGG Oh, my Gawd.

CHARLIE (*Playing for time.*) I feel a song coming on. (*Singing to* JUGG.) 'When Irish eyes are in the library–this is Billy here–and Rupert's in the cabinet–so push off out of here'.

(BILLY *goes to drink again.*)

CHARLIE (*Quickly to* BILLY, *singing.*) 'Drink no more, my Billy' (*To the tune of 'Weep no More, my Lady'.*)

BILLY Just a sip.

CHARLIE Sign first.

HARDCASTLE Let him have his drink if he wants to. Propose a toast.

BILLY Aye. Here's to . . . to . . . woof woof.

(BILLY *suddenly barks twice and passes out under table down* R.)

HARDCASTLE What's he playing at now? If I don't get this signed now, Barnet, I'll leave all my money to the Battersea Dog's house.

(BILLY *head pops up, with tongue out and subsides.*)

CHARLIE I'll take 'im out for a walk. He ain't been out at all, today.

BILLY Woof, Woof, Woof.

(CHARLIE *pushes* BILLY, *who is on his knees, out of french windows.*)

HARDCASTLE By gum, I've had enough . . . I'm not giving ten thousand pounds to a man, who can't hold his liquor.

BILLY (*Off.*) Woof-woof!

HARDCASTLE Look at him now, he's half way up that lamp-post.

CYNTHIA Now, don't go off the deep end.

HARDCASTLE And you're not marrying a raving lunatic. It's all off. He'll get nowt.

(CHARLIE *re-enters french windows.*)

CHARLIE Eh?

HARDCASTLE Nowt! D'you hear me, Barnet? Piper give us a push into ballroom. I'm going to have a basin full of this punch that's been having such a devastating effect on everybody.

(PIPER *pushes him out.* CYNTHIA *follows.* CHARLIE *and* JUGG *sit down dejectedly on settee. Music from ballroom 'Dramatic Moderne'.*)

CHARLIE I haven't even got me fare 'ome.

JUGG Don't worry, Mr B. If it comes to the push, I can let you have a few bob.

CHARLIE I'm thinking about Hardcastle.

JUGG Hardcastle will have changed his mind tomorrow.

CHARLIE And by tomorrow he'll have found out about my Hickory Woods. I've gotta get that agreement signed tonight.

JUGG Old Piper's got the agreement safely clutched in that briefcase of his.

CHARLIE Piper. Do you think we can get him to champion our cause?

JUGG Of course we couldn't. Although Miss Amy could wrap him round her little finger.

CHARLIE That's it then. We'll have to get her in on our side.

JUGG I'm afraid not. She's unconscious.

CHARLIE Well wake her up.

JUGG I can't wake her up.

CHARLIE Why not?

JUGG I accidently nobbled her with a glass of punch.

CHARLIE You have a positive mania for nobbling the wrong people.

JUGG She's laying flat on her back in her boudoir.

CHARLIE Eh!

JUGG And Gawd knows when she'll come round.

CHARLIE Bang goes our last chance.

JUGG Unless we could get someone to dress up as Aunt Amy. I mean Piper's shortsighted–and if I nicked his glasses.

CHARLIE And gave him a couple of stiff brandies.

JUGG Yes. All we need is someone to impersonate Miss Amy.

(*There is a pause as they look at each other. Fade music from ballroom.*)

JUGG (*Quickly sagging.*) I'm too small.

CHARLIE (*Standing on tiptoe.*) Well I'm too tall.

JUGG What we need is someone with a high-pitched voice–

CHARLIE And a slight North Country accent.

BILLY (*Off.*) Charlie!

(BILLY *staggers in from the garden.*)

BILLY Charlie.

(CHARLIE *and* JUGG *look at each other and nod.*)

JUGG I'll go and borrow one of Miss Amy's dresses.

(JUGG *exits hall downstage.*)

BILLY What's going on now?

CHARLIE You're going in for a little fancy-dress competition.

BILLY Am I!

CHARLIE Yes. You're going to dress up. As Aunt Amy.

BILLY I can't do that. I don't look like a woman.

CHARLIE 'Course you do. You've got your mother's features.

BILLY Aye–and me father's fixtures.

CHARLIE (*Pushing* BILLY.) Get in the library and get your clothes off.

(*He pushes* BILLY *into the library.* CYNTHIA *enters from the hall upstage.*)

CYNTHIA I'm sorry, Mr Barnet. I can't get Daddy to change his mind.

CHARLIE Don't worry. We've got a little scheme afoot. Billy's dressing up as Aunt Amy to get Piper to get the agreement so I can get the money.

CYNTHIA It sounds very complicated.

CHARLIE We can't do things the easy way.

(JUGG *enters from the hall downstage with duplicate of* AMY'S *evening dress.*)

JUGG Here we are, Mr B. It's the nearest match I could find.

(CHARLIE *takes dress.*)

CHARLIE Marvellous!

JUGG All I've got to do now is to give Piper a couple of quick doubles.

CHARLIE Here we are, Jugg–

(CHARLIE *goes to his pocket.*)

JUGG No, no, have this one on me.

(JUGG *goes into library.*)

CHARLIE All right, Miss Cynthia, you keep watch here. I'll go and give Billy his instructions.

(WINNIE *comes in from library.*)

WINNIE Why's my Billy changing into his underpants?

CHARLIE Rehearsing.

WINNIE What for?

CHARLIE Orpheus in the underwear.

WINNIE Oh. Here, that Michael's coming round.

CHARLIE — Michael's coming round! Where's my brass shillalegh?

(CHARLIE *takes warming pan from* D.R. *and exits library followed by* WINNIE. *The cocktail cabinet opens and* RUPERT (Double) *staggers out.* CYNTHIA *rushes over.*)

CYNTHIA — No, darling. You stay in there, my pet.

(*She pushes him back as* HARDCASTLE *enters from hall upstage.*)

HARDCASTLE — By gum, lass, it were a sorry day for me when I thought of this damn fool idea. Ten thousand pounds! If I'd been in my right mind, I'd have never done it.

(*From the library comes the sound of 'Gong'.*)

What was that?

CYNTHIA — The library clock again.

HARDCASTLE — It makes a devil of a row for a clock we haven't got.

(*The cocktail cabinet opens and* RUPERT (Double) *Starts to stagger out backwards.* CYNTHIA *pushes him back. There is a loud crash and* CYNTHIA *hurriedly shuts the door.*)

HARDCASTLE — What's that?

(*There are bumps and crashes from within the cabinet.*)

CYNTHIA — I can't hear anything.

(*Pause. There is another loud crash.*)

HARDCASTLE — (*Listening to all the racket.*) Can't you?

(*There is the small sound of one glass breaking.*)

CYNTHIA — No.

HARDCASTLE — I'm going off me rocker. Push us into the ballroom–I'm going to have a couple of quick'uns before they lock me up.

(CYNTHIA *pushes him off* L. *of hall upstage.* CHARLIE'S *head appears round the library door.*)

CHARLIE (*Into library.*) Ready?

BILLY (*Off.*) Aye. There's no one out there is there?

CHARLIE Now–just you do as I told you. Jugg's gone off to get Piper. I'll 'ang around in the garden.

(CHARLIE *exits by french windows.* BILLY *enters reluctantly dressed as* AMY, *with a stole over his head. He crosses and sits on settee, tripping over his long skirts on the way. Feeling the need to mop his brow, he lifts up his skirt, showing his rolled-up trousers, and takes a handkerchief from his pocket. As part of his disguise as* AMY *he has a fringe of hair on an elastic band round his forehead, this he moves down under his chin while he mops his brow. He looks down at the fringe and mimes stroking a beard, then moves fringe to his upper lip and twirls it as a moustache. While he is enjoying this little 'game'* PIPER *enters behind him, wearing a party hat and carrying a glass of brandy. He thinks he sees* AMY, *and an amorous glow comes into his eyes. He places the glass on the table up* C., *stealthily approaches* BILLY *and sits beside him.*)

PIPER Hullo!

(BILLY *reacts and quickly pushes his skirt over his knees and puts fringe back in place.*)

PIPER Amy, so we are alone a last!

BILLY (*High-pitched voice.*) What about that agreement–

PIPER Oh, no, pleasure before business.

(PIPER *runs his fingers down* AMY'S *knee. Playfully.*) EE-nee-meeny-miney-mo.

BILLY That's as far as you can go!

(BILLY *slaps his hand.*)

PIPER Oh, we're feeling playful tonight, are we?

(PIPER *playfully nudges* BILLY.)

BILLY (*Nudging him back.*) Oh, no!

PIPER (*Nudging* BILLY.) Oh, yes!

BILLY (*Nudging* PIPER.) Oh, no!

PIPER (*Nudging* BILLY.) Oh, yes, we are!

BILLY Oh, no we're not!

(BILLY *gives* PIPER *a big nudge and* PIPER *falls to the floor.*)

PIPER Oh, you've got the devil in you tonight and so have I.

(*He starts to chase* BILLY *round the room.* BILLY *and* PIPER *fall into a heap on settee.* HARDCASTLE *enters from hall upstage.*)

HARDCASTLE (*Grinning.*) Piper! Piper! Don't worry, Amy. He'll have to marry you now.

(HARDCASTLE *exits upstage.* BILLY *leaps over* PIPER *and settee and flees round the room with* PIPER *in hot pursuit.* BILLY *eventually evades him by pulling a shawl over his head and* PIPER *pulls back panel (detachable) of* BILLY'S *evening-dress.* BILLY *exits through the french windows.*)

PIPER (*Holding the back panel of* BILLY'S *dress.*) Amy, Amy, come back, come back.

(PIPER *exits through the french windows.* AMY *enters from hall downstage crossing to french windows.* BILLY *appears from french windows heading for library door–They both do a double-take and scream on seeing each other and* BILLY *rushes off into the library.*)

AMY Oh, I'm still not right, I'm seeing things.

(PIPER *re-enters from french windows.*)

PIPER (*Seeing* AMY.) Ah-ha! Amy!

AMY Ah!

(PIPER *with arms outstretched stealthily approaches her.*)

AMY (*Utterly amazed.*) Arnold, what is it?

PIPER I want my reward.

(*He grabs her.*)

AMY Arnold, you're intoxicated . . .

PIPER Yes. I'm intoxicated with you . . . (*He goes to archway.*) Oh! Amy, Amy (*Singing.*) Oh Amy, 'My Heart's on Fire. The flames grow higher'.

(PIPER, *dancing, exits into hall upstage.*)

AMY (*Murmuring.*) Ah, Arnold.

(CHARLIE *enters from french windows.* AMY *has her back to* CHARLIE.)

CHARLIE Piper's gone, 'as'e? Good, get your clothes off.

AMY P-pardon?

CHARLIE Come on, we can't waste time. (*He smacks her bottom.*)

AMY Oh!

CHARLIE We gotta get on with it. (CHARLIE *goes to grab her and she slaps his hand.*) Don't you come that lark with me or I'll give you a four-penny one.

AMY Oh!

CHARLIE Get your dress off, first.

AMY Oh!

CHARLIE Well, nobody's goin' to see your woolly pants.

AMY Oh!

(*She faints into* CHARLIE'S *arms.)*

CHARLIE (*Realizing it's* AMY.) The wrong version. (*He picks her up and carries her to the cocktail cabinet.* RUPERT *comes out holding whisky bottle.*)

RUPERT (*Sees* AMY'S *posterior.*) Oh, bottom's up.

(RUPERT *returns to cabinet.* CHARLIE *carries her towards hallway as* JUGG *enters hall upstage.*)

CHARLIE (*To* JUGG.) One bag of household nuts.

(CHARLES *exits hallway downstage with* AMY.)

JUGG (*To himself.*) I 'ope somebody will come and see us on visiting days.

(CYNTHIA *enters* R. *of hall upstage.*)

CYNTHIA Jugg, whatever's the matter?

JUGG I think I'm going to be head butler at Wormwood Scrubs.

(JUGG *exits library.* CHARLIE *re-enters from hall downstage.*)

CHARLIE Well, that's got rid of her.

CYNTHIA (*To* CHARLIE.) How did Billy get on as Aunt Amy?

CHARLIE (*Sarcastically.*) Oh, very well. They're practically on their honeymoon.

CYNTHIA It's good thing Mr Piper's shortsighted.

CHARLIE Anyway thank Gawd Michael's out of the way.

CYNTHIA But he isn't. Michael's drinking with Daddy in the ballroom.

MICHAEL (*Off in Yorkshire.*) EEee–Mr 'Ardcastle, that's a right good 'un.

CHARLIE (*Aside to* CYNTHIA.) Michael?

(Cynthia *nods.* MICHAEL *enters from hall upstage pushing* HARDCASTLE. *Piper follows.*)

MICHAEL (*To* CHARLIE.) Nearly, there, me boyo!

CHARLIE (*Aside to* MICHAEL.) What 'ave you done with Winnie?

MICHAEL (*Aside in Irish.*) She's in the library a trifle tied up.

CHARLIE At any other time I'd be grateful.

HARDCASTLE Your Billy had me fooled, Barnet. I thought he couldn't hold his drink. (*To* MICHAEL.) Sign that agreement and then the pair of us will get roaring drunk.

(*They cross to table.*)

MICHAEL (*Yorkshire.*) I'm going to sign, Charlie.

(PIPER *takes out money.*)

CHARLIE Pax! 'old it! Feignights!

HARDCASTLE What's the matter now?

CYNTHIA (*By french windows.*) Look–a falling star!

HARDCASTLE I don't care if the whole world's falling apart–let's get this signed.

CYNTHIA No, Billy and I should wish on it for luck.

MICHAEL (*Irish.*) I'll sign first.

CHARLIE (*Pulling him.*) You'll wish first.

(CHARLIE *grabs pen and moves to chest.* MICHAEL *follows,* CHARLIE *turns to see if* HARDCASTLE *is looking, then deftly lifts the lid of the chest and boots* MICHAEL *in. He bangs the lid down.* CHARLIE *and* CYNTHIA *sit on chest.*)

HARDCASTLE (*Looking up.*) Where's Hickory Wood?

CHARLIE He's having a bit of chest trouble.

HARDCASTLE Has he gone out?

CHARLIE I 'ope so!

CYNTHIA I'll–er I'll go and find him for you.

(CYNTHIA *exits from french windows upstage.* BILLY *enters from library.*)

HARDCASTLE (*Looking out of french windows.*) Billy! Billy! Billy!

BILLY (*Behind* HARDCASTLE.) 'Ullo.

HARDCASTLE How'd you get there?

BILLY I walked from there to here.

HARDCASTLE For the last time let's get this agreement signed–don't say you've lost the agreement again? Piper.

PIPER Oh, dear! Never mind, I'll have to use the duplicate copy. I'll just read the clauses you have to sign.

(*The cocktail cabinet starts to open.* CHARLIE *dashes over and leans on it.*)

... Providing there are no other living relatives–if you'll just sign there.

(*The lid of the chest starts to open and* CHARLIE *dashes from cocktail cabinet to sit on it.*)

HARDCASTLE (*Looking up.*) Barnet will you keep still? Come over 'ere and have a drink.

(*He hands* CHARLIE *drink from table.*)

CHARLIE (*Drinking it.*) Just a quick one–all time for.

HARDCASTLE That's the drink that put Billy under the table.

(CHARLIE *splutters. Goes to return to the chest, but collapses out of french windows.*)

PIPER One last initial here–

(*The lid of the chest opens and* MICHAEL (Double) *starts to get out.* BILLY *jumps up, dashing over and sits on it.*)

HARDCASTLE Where . . . ? Come back here.

(PIPER *wheels* HARDCASTLE *over to* BILLY. *The cabinet door opens and* RUPERT'S (Double) *arm appears.* BILLY *dashes over and leans against it with a look of horror on his face.*)

HARDCASTLE What the blazes are you doing?

(PIPER *pushes* HARDCASTLE *towards cabinet. The lid of the chest opens and* BILLY *dashes back.*)

HARDCASTLE Keep still!

(PIPER *pushes* HARDCASTLE *towards chest as the cabinet door opens again.* BILLY *sets off in that direction. The chest opens and this time* HARDCASTLE *sees it.*)

HARDCASTLE What the . . . ?

(*He looks inside and shoots completely out of his chair. In doing so he bangs the lid down on* MICHAEL'S (Double) *head and sits on the chest.*)

HARDCASTLE (*Sitting on lid.*) I'm seeing double. (*Pointing to cabinet.*) Get me a brandy, Piper.

(PIPER *moves to cabinet.* BILLY *is standing there with a look of horror on his face. Suddenly* BILLY *dashes out of french windows.*)

BILLY Charlie! Charlie!!

(PIPER *opens cabinet door and then shuts it quickly. He looks out of french windows, opens the cabinet door and shuts it again.*)

PIPER Mr. Har-Har-Har-Har . . .

HARDCASTLE What are you laughing at–? Get the brandy.

PIPER I think I need one myself.

(PIPER *timorously goes to open cabinet, but* RUPERT *comes out a little unsteadily.*)

RUPERT Good evening, good evening. Good night. (*He sees them, bows, and returns into cabinet.* PIPER *and* HARDCASTLE *gape at each other.*)

HARDCASTLE Piper did you see what I thought I saw?

PIPER (*Mouth open.*) What did you think you thought you saw?

HARDCASTLE I think I thought I saw Billy just rush out into the garden.

PIPER So did I!

HARDCASTLE Then who the blazes is in there?

(*The lid of the chest starts bumping* HARDCASTLE *up and down.*)

PIPER Oh. You're shaking, Mr Hardcastle.

(HARDCASTLE *jumps up, the chest opens and* MICHAEL *staggers out.*)

HARDCASTLE (*Sinking into wheelchair.*) Great balls of fire!

MICHAEL (*Rubbing head.*) Oh–somebody's been hitting me with a shillelagh. Now where's the drinks?

(MICHAEL *staggers to cocktail cabinet and lurches in. There is a loud crash.*)

HARDCASTLE That makes two of them in there.

PIPER Do you think we are suffering from hallucinations?

HARDCASTLE We'll soon find out – one of us open that door!

(CHARLIE *drags* BILLY *in from garden.*)

BILLY No. No, Charlie.

CHARLIE Well, I've found him wandering about in the garden, silly boy.

(HARDCASTLE *and* PIPER *are horrified.*)

BILLY You don't understand, Charlie.

CHARLIE Now, now William. Leave it to me. You've still got to sign the agreement.

HARDCASTLE What about the other two?

CHARLIE What other two?

HARDCASTLE The other two lunatics staggering about looking like this lunatic.

CHARLIE You mean–

(CHARLIE *dashes to the chest and looks in.*)

CHARLIE He's gone!

PIPER (*Indicating the cabinet.*) He's in there.

CHARLIE But what about . . . ?

HARDCASTLE He's in there too. Barnet, open that door!

CHARLIE This one? Over here?

(CHARLIE *weakly goes to the cabinet and opens the door.* RUPERT *and* MICHAEL (Doubles) *fall out backwards into heap. They are masked by the settee.* CYNTHIA *enters french windows.*)

CYNTHIA Mr Barnet, I can't find Billy anywhere–Oh!

HARDCASTLE Cynthia, do you know anything about these two jokers?

CYNTHIA (*Stepping over* Doubles.) Well, yes–I'm engaged to this one on the left.

HARDCASTLE So that's Billy?

CYNTHIA No, Rupert.

HARDCASTLE I suppose that must be Billy?

CHARLIE No, Michael.

(BILLY *giggles.*)

HARDCASTLE (*To* BILLY.) What are you laughing at?

BILLY I'm Billy.

HARDCASTLE I thought you were a lunatic–it must be me.

(WINNIE *comes in from library, she is gagged and her hands are tied.*)

HARDCASTLE I suppose this is their sister?

WINNIE (*Removing gag.*) Where's that Michael?

HARDCASTLE Take your pick.

WINNIE (*To* BILLY.) Oh, Billy. (*To* CHARLIE.) I suppose he is my Billy, isn't he?

CHARLIE Two and two?

BILLY Five.

CHARLIE Yes! (CHARLIE *nods.*)

(BILLY *and* WINNIE *embrace.* JUGG *enters from hall downstage.*)

JUGG Excuse me, sir. (*Taking in situation.*) Excuse me, sir. (*He moves to go.*)

(BILLY *steps outside french windows and is replaced by* (Double) *who stands with his back to the audience embracing* WINNIE.)

[Note. JUGG *must make a big entrance and reaction to cover the change over.*]

HARDCASTLE Come here, Jugg. Do you know anything about this gathering of the Hickory Wood tribe?

JUGG Not a thing, sir.

HARDCASTLE What about that Barnet, is he in on it too?

CHARLIE Well–

(Jugg *slips* CHARLIE *a pound note.*)

Well,–

(JUGG *slips him another pound note.*)

Er–

(JUGG *gives him his wallet.*)

HARDCASTLE I don't believe it.

JUGG Sir.

HARDCASTLE Jugg, you're sacked.

JUGG Thank you, sir. Same time in the morning, sir.

HARDCASTLE Aye.

(JUGG *exits hall upstage.*)

HARDCASTLE Piper, take this down ... To Billy Hickory Wood–Ten thousand pounds. To Rupert Hickory Wood–Ten thousand pounds. To Michael Hickory Wood–ten thousand pounds. That makes thirty thousand pounds. By gum, Piper, I'm right glad there's only three of them.

(JUGG *enters hall upstage followed by a young man with out-stretched hand.*)

YOUNG MAN Bon soir–je suis Pierre Hickory Wood ... –

(*It is another identical brother. He kisses* HARDCASTLE *on both cheeks.*)

CHAOS!!!

CURTAIN

LIGHTING PLOT

USED AT THE WHITEHALL THEATRE, LONDON

Note: The following abbreviations have been used:

F.O.H. = Front of House.
O.W. = Open White.
A.A. = Acting Area.

Property Fittings Required (All Practical).

4 pairs electric-candle wall-brackets.
2 single wall-brackets.
Fairy lights — french window backing.
Door light — cocktail cabinet.
Strip light — above picture — Up Centre.

Interior:
Lounge in Jonathan Hardcastle's country house.
The same scene throughout and the action is continuous.

GENERAL SETTING

		Colour No.
1. Floats — Pink — White. On check at 7½		
2. Batten No. 1 — Pink — White. Full Up		52,54
3. Setting of Spot Batten (Numbering from left prompt side)		
No. 1.	French window — Up Left Centre	54
No. 2 A.A.	On settle — Down Left	54
No. 3 A.A.	Centre stage — Centre	54
No. 4.	Table left of arm-chair — Down Right Centre	54
No. 5.	Refectory table — Down Right	54
No. 6.	On arch — Up Right	54
No. 7.	On bureau — Down Left	54
No. 8.	On library door — Right Centre	54
No. 9.	Arm-chair — Down Right Centre	54
No. 10	On wing chair — Up Centre	54
No. 11 A.A.	Down centre — Down Centre	54
	(All Full Up.)	

4. Setting of F.O.H. Spots (Numbering from the top) Prompt side		*Colour* No.
No. 1.	Cocktail cabinet — Down Left	O.W.
No. 2.	Centre of large carpet — Centre Stage	O.W.
No. 3.	Arm-chair — Down Right	O.W.
No. 4.	1 foot O.P. off Centre — Up Right Centre	O.W.
No. 5.	Refectory table — Down Right	O.W.
No. 6.	Screen — Up Right Centre	51
O.P. side		
No. 1.	Refectory table — Down Right	O.W.
No. 2.	Floats-down stage to P.S. side — Down Centre	O.W.
No. 3.	Cocktail cabinet — Down Left	O.W.
No. 4.	Prompt side pillar — Up Left Centre	O.W.
No. 5.	Cocktail cabinet — Down Left	O.W.
No. 6.	Small table — Up Centre	51
	(All Full Up.)	

5. 2 Patt. 123. Set behind prompt side pillar on boom bar	*Colour* No.
Upper — Downstage of hall arch	52
Lower — Wing chair	52
6. 2 Patt. 123. Set behind O.P. pillar on boom bar	
Upper — downstage of chest	52
Lower — bottom of screen	52

7.	1 flood — french window backing	18
	1 spot — french window backing	17
	1 flood — library door backing	54
	3 1,000 stage floods — hall backing	52
	1 spot — above hall arch	52
	Hanging ground row — french window backing	18
	Practical door light — cocktail cabinet	Amber
	1 length — cocktail cabinet	Orange

No cues in ACT ONE OR TWO.

Cue No. 1. Act Three Page 93
On Billy's 'Well... you see, Winnie says I've got to tell... Blackout everything on master switch except french window backing flood and ground row. Cocktail cabinet practical light — orange.

Cue No. 2. Page 93.
On Piper's 'It's all right I've found the switch'. Everything full up to end of play.

EFFECTS PLOT

Act One

Cue 1: page 1. As curtain rises. 2 front doorbells from upstage of hall.
Cue 2: page 1. On Cynthia's 'At this rate'. 1 front doorbell.
Cue 3: page 1. On Amy's 'Now where was I?' 1 front doorbell.
Cue 4: page 2. On Jugg's stamp down left — bureau. Bureau drawer flies open.
Cue 5: page 4. As Hardcastle's stick hits floor. Bureau drawer flies open.
Cue 6: page 6. On Jugg's 'It's their early closing day'. 1 front doorbell.
Cue 7: page 7. On Hardcastle's 'She does stop talking sometimes'. 1 front doorbell.
Cue 8: page 14. As Jugg drinks brandy down left. 2 front doorbells.
Cue 9: page 24. As Rupert drops case. Bureau drawer flies open.
Cue 10: page 35. As Rupert drops case. Bureau drawer flies open.

Act Two

Cue 11: page 51. As Rupert blows down horn. Bassoon sound — off left.
Cue 12: page 61. As Billy stamps on floor near bureau. Bureau flies open during dance.
Cue 13: page 74. On Rupert's exit into cocktail cabinet. Loud crash (No. 1).
Cue 14: page 79. On Rupert's exit into cocktail cabinet. Loud crash (No. 2).

Act Three

Cue 15: page 88. On Hardcastle's line 'You'll be hearing things next'. Loud thud — off left.
Cue 16: page 90. As Charlie's shovel crashes on to Piper's head — loud thud — off left.
Cue 17: Page 93. As Billy's (Double) exits into cocktail cabinet — loud crash (No. 3). In blackout.
Cue 18: page 98. As Jugg stamps down left. Bureau drawer flies out.
Cue 19: page 106. On Rupert's exit into cocktail cabinet. Loud crash (No. 4).
Cue 20: page 108. On Hardcastle's line 'He's right struck on you'. Loud gong — down right.
Cue 21: page 114. On Hardcastle's line 'I'd have never done it'. Loud gong — down right.
Cue 22: page 114. As Cynthia pushes Rupert (Double) into cocktail cabinet — 4 loud crashes.
Cue 23: page 122. As Michael exits into cocktail cabinet. Loud crash.

FURNITURE AND PROPERTY PLOT

Throughout the Play:
Carpet centre stage.
Small rug — below screen up centre.
Long curtains at french windows and archway.

1. Refectory table — down right.
   Large white tablecloth. Two candelabras.
   On it: Coffee urn, cup and saucers, small hand bell, 3 brandy glasses, 'Alka Seltzer' bottle (full — large peppermints used), syphon, vase of flowers, cigarette-box (empty), ashtray, 2 boxes matches, packet of 20 cigarettes. Party dressing.
2. Large picture — on wall above refectory table.
3. Small stool — downstage of refectory table.
4. Arm-chair — down right centre. With footstool and 2 cushions.
5. Small table — left of arm-chair.
   On it: Magazines, small book.
6. Large screen — movable for Act Three. Prop shovel set on hook behind it.
7. Wing chair — set with back to audience.
8. Small table — left of wing chair.
   On it: Vase of roses, fruit bowl with bananas and oranges, telephone, brandy glass (half full for Jugg), telephone directory, ashtray (full on top of telephone book).

9. Fire-irons — left of fire.place — poker and shovel.
10. Large chest — up left centre.
On it: large shawl — set for Act Two.
Inside it: Bin for Cigarette-ends.
11. Fireplace — up centre — clock, ashtray, letters, fender.
12. Cocktail cabinet. Set inside it: Ice bucket, soda syphon, bottle of brandy, gin, whisky, full bottle of gin. 2 brandy glasses (half full). Assorted glasses — dressing.
13. Settee — left centre.
On it: 2 cushions, painted canvas — Cynthia.
14. Bureau — down left. Trick drawer. Operated from behind flat.
On it: Old-fashioned gramophone horn — detachable — records set on gramophone — ashtray — 2 boxes of matches — vase of flowers.
In drawer: 2 cigars — cut.
15. Pedestal — above bureau.
16. Warming pan — downstage of library door.
17. 2 crossed swords — practical — on wall above chest.
18. Light switch — set of three — downstage of library door.
19. Paintings — dressing on both downstage walls and hall backing.
20. Doors closed.
21. French window open.

Details of Music Used in the London Production

MUSIC PLOT

PAGE	NAME	PAXTON NUMBER	VOLUME	SPEAKER
Pre-curtain	Busy day	P.R.717		F.O.H.
Music	Bella Vista	P.R.717		”
	Preview	P.R.609		”
	First Fling	P.R.658		”
	Midsummer mood	P.R.620		”
	Touch and Go	P.R.658		”
	Leaps and Bounds	P.R.725		”
	Stockholm Polka	P.R.688		”
	Le Cabaret	P.R.406		”
	'One for the Pot'	—		”
	(Intro. 2 mins.)	—		”

* All records from W. Paxton and Co. Ltd., 36 Dean Street, W.1.

PAGE	NAME	PAXTON NUMBER	VOLUME	SPEAKER
	'Queen'	—		F.O.H.
ACT ONE	'One for The Pot' *(Intro. 30 secs.)*	—		”
	High Society	P.R.732		O.P.
	Happy Man	P.R.732		”
	Sixes and Sevens	P.R.731		”
	The Chase	P.R.731		”
	High Society	P.R.732		”
Interval	Parade of the Bottles	P.R.722		F.O.H.
	Early Riser	P.R.720		”
	'Chico'	P.R.621		O.P.
	Pink Gin	P.R.697		”
ACT II	'One for The Pot' *(Intro. 30 secs.)*	—		F.O.H
	Mood Moderene	P.R.732		O.P.
	Waltz	—		”
	Chooka Chooka	P.R.730		”
	Fling	—		P.S.
	Tango 'Jealousy'	—		”
	Mood Blue	P.R.732		”
	The Chase	P.R.731		”

Interval	Cheerful Chatter	P.R.688	F.O.H.
	Bubble Bath	P.R.697	"
	Samba Sam	P.R.621	"
	Angel Cake	P.R.609	"
	Let's Play	PR.406	"
Act Three	'One for The Pot' (*Intro. 30 secs.)*	—	"
	Trumpet	P.R.731	O.P.
	Dramatic Moderne	P.R.731	"
	Theme Music for Play Out	—	F.O.H.

SETTING — PROPERTY PLOT

Act One — Off Right

Upstage of Hall

1. Large birthday cake — Amy.
2. Assorted coats and wraps — Cynthia.
3. Abstract portrait of Cynthia — Cynthia.
4. Suitcase — large — Amy.
5. Briefcase: *in it:* pen, several agreements, newspaper cuttings, £10,000 in £5 notes — Piper.
6. Pallette — with 2 clip-on pots of red and black paint — Amy.
7. Cloth on pallette — Amy.
8. 3 large paint brushes — Amy.
9. Large canvas paper both sides — Amy.
10. Small hand-case — Hickory Wood.
11. Briefcase — Charlie.
12. Umbrella — Charlie.

Downstage of Hall

13. Wheelchair:
    (*a*) Trick arms — Hardcastle.
    Whisky in R. arm.
    Soda in L. arm.
    (*b*) Rug }
    (*c*) Stick } Hardcastle
    (*d*) Plastic glass }

Library Door. 2 dress-suits — props for Weaver and Double — Jugg.

Act One — Off Left — French Windows

1. Suitcase — Rupert.
2. Doubles dress-suit — Double 1.
3. Easel — Cynthia.
5. Brass poker — bent — Jugg.
6. Bowler hat — bent — Charlie.

Act Two

Strike:

1. Pallette and cloth — table D.R.
2. Bin in chest.

Set:

1. Magazines — table D.R. to lower shelf.
2. Small chair — behind screen — to cover trap-door.
3. Set Rupert's suitcase — under bureau D. left.
4. Make coffee — reset table D.R.
5. Ashtray off telephone book U.C
6. Two crashes — prompt side.

Act Two Off Right

1. Cardboard box' — raffle tickets — Amy.
2. Knitting bag — Piper.
4. Charlie's dress-suit, check money in wallet £2 — Jugg.
5. Evening wrap — Cynthia.

Act Three

Strike:

Syphon, banana, bottles, Alka Seltzer D.R.
3 Brandy glasses D.R.
Coffee cup and small handbell U.C
Picture behind chair D.R.
Ashtray off bureau D.L.

Set:

Arm-chair and table over 6 in. D.R.
Charlie's hunting suit, plimsolls, etc., behind screen.
Hickory Wood's evening-suit off R.
Fire-irons U.C.
Cigarette-box — re-set U.S. table.
2 boxes of matches table D.R.
Reset cushions to centre on settee:
Unpin L.C. side of runner.
Block U.S. arch for Jugg.

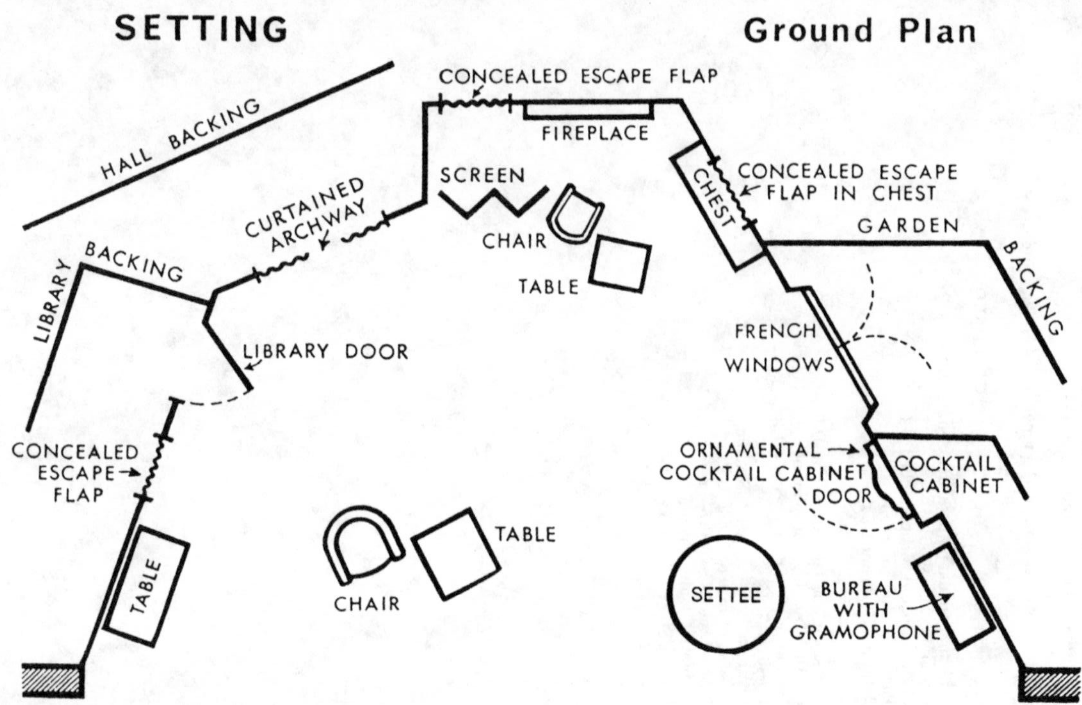
SETTING
Ground Plan
HALL BACKING
CONCEALED ESCAPE FLAP
FIREPLACE
SCREEN
CHAIR
TABLE
CONCEALED ESCAPE FLAP IN CHEST
CHEST
GARDEN
BACKING
CURTAINED ARCHWAY
LIBRARY
BACKING
LIBRARY DOOR
FRENCH WINDOWS
CONCEALED ESCAPE FLAP
ORNAMENTAL COCKTAIL CABINET DOOR
COCKTAIL CABINET
TABLE
CHAIR
TABLE
SETTEE
BUREAU WITH GRAMOPHONE

DIAGRAM SHOWING 'DOUBLES' ESCAPE ROUTE (Act Two)

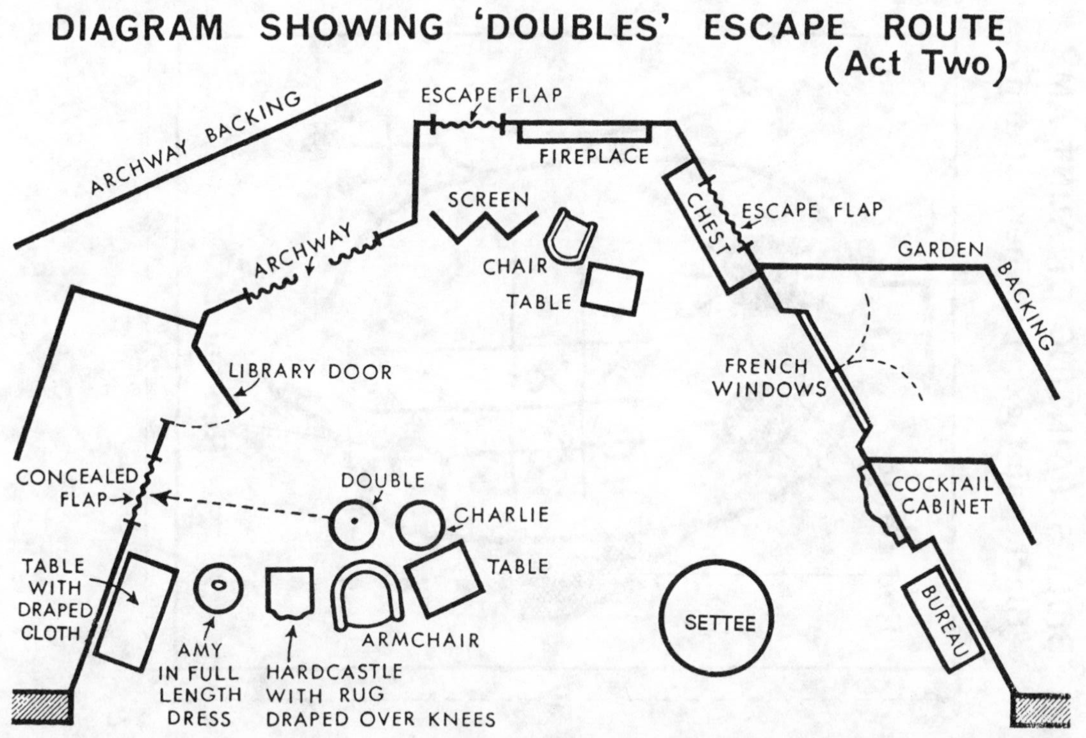

BILLY'S PAINTING OF AUNT AMY
(Black paint except where stated)

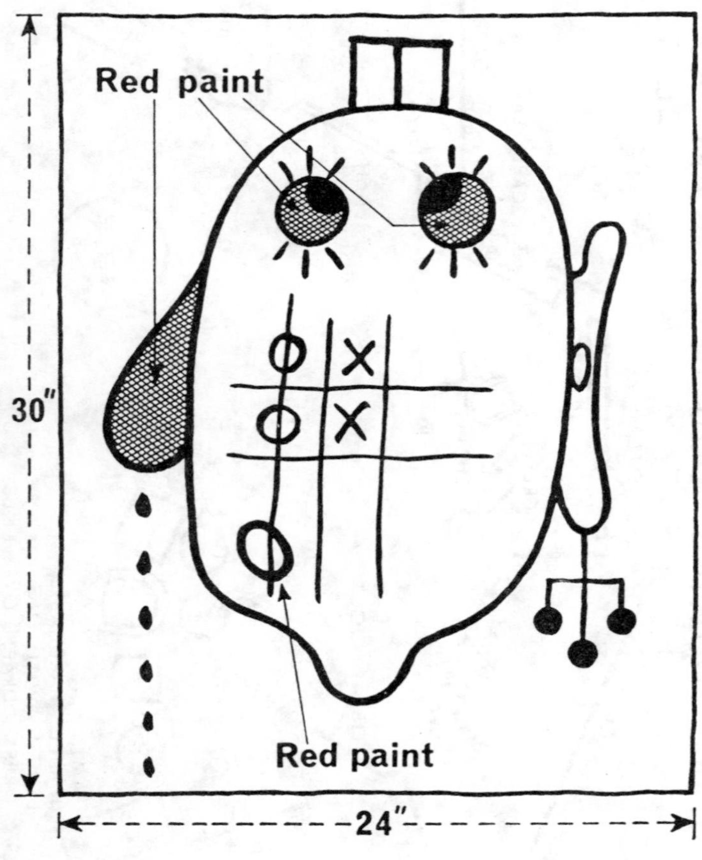